The Sweet Magnolias Cookbook

#1 *New York Times* Bestselling Author
SHERRYL WOODS

with Chef Teddi Wohlford

MORE THAN 150 FAVORITE SOUTHERN RECIPES

NETFLIX
SWEET MAGNOLIAS
NOW ON NETFLIX

Recycling programs
for this product may
not exist in your area.

ISBN-13: 978-0-7783-8628-5

The Sweet Magnolias Cookbook

First published in 2012. This edition published in 2022 with revised text.

This edition published by arrangement with Harlequin Books S.A.

For questions and comments about the quality of this book, please contact us at
CustomerService@Harlequin.com.

Mira
22 Adelaide St. West, 41st Floor
Toronto, Ontario M5H 4E3, Canada
BookClubbish.com

Printed in Italy by Grafica Veneta.

THE SWEET MAGNOLIAS SERIES BY
#1 *NEW YORK TIMES* BESTSELLING AUTHOR
SHERRYL WOODS

Stealing Home

A Slice of Heaven

Feels Like Family

Welcome to Serenity

Home in Carolina

Sweet Tea at Sunrise

Honeysuckle Summer

Midnight Promises

Catching Fireflies

Where Azaleas Bloom

Swan Point

For a complete list of all titles
by Sherryl Woods, visit
WWW.SHERRYLWOODS.COM.

Contents

Introduction. xi

SWEET MAGNOLIAS MARGARITA NIGHTS (& OTHER COCKTAILS AND MUNCHIES!)

Helen's Lethal Margaritas 3

Dana Sue's Killer Chunky Guacamole 4

Magnolia Blossom Cocktail. 6

Snow Cream Martinis 6

Mint Juleps. 7

Citrus Bourbon Slushy 8

Fire & Ice Pickles 9

C'mon, Baby, Light My Fire Chicken Wings 10

Cheddar Blossoms 12

Blue Cheese Dressing with Cognac 13

SULLIVAN'S RESTAURANT SPECIALTIES OF THE HOUSE

Toasted Pecan & Red Pepper Jam 17

Garlic Toast Rounds 18

Bacon & Swiss Appetizer Cheesecake 19

Shrimp, Crab & Swiss Appetizer Cheesecake 20

Cheddar Corn Muffins 21

Corn Muffin Mix 21

Navy Bean Soup. 22

Lowcountry She-Crab Soup 23

Gullah Peanut & Sweet Potato Soup 24

Sherried Mushroom Soup 25

Baby Greens with Pears, Blue Cheese & Toasted Walnut Vinaigrette 26

Citrus Salmon with Crunchy Crumb Topping 27

Sea Bass with Vegetables & Herbs en Papillote 28

Herb Cheese Spread 30

Bourbon & Brown Sugar Grilled Salmon with Tropical Fruit Salsa 31

Sweet & Tangy Tomato-Basil Vinaigrette 33

Shrimp Scampi Linguine 35

Panfried Catfish with Spicy Cornmeal Coating 36

Pan-Seared Trout with Browned Butter & Lemon Sauce 38

Peachy Grilled Chicken with Spicy Peanut Sauce 39

Honey Grilled Pork Tenderloin with Peach Salsa. 41

Roasted Spring Lamb with Herbs & Madeira Sauce. 42

"Oven-Fried" Chicken Tenders 43

Garlic & Rosemary Roasted Pork Loin with Sour Cream
& Mushroom Sauce 44

Vegetarian Pasta Primavera with Smoked Gouda Sauce. 45

Mixed Mushroom Risotto 46

Three-Cheese Macaroni Casserole. 49

Southern-Style Green Beans Amandine with Frizzled Bacon
& Smoked Almonds 50

Carolina Red Rice 51

Sweet Potato Soufflé with Pecan & Oat Streusel Topping 52

Walnut-Crusted Potatoes with Herbs. 53

SERENITY FARMERS' MARKET

Pickled Green Tomatoes 57

Dana Sue's Pickled Okra 58

Pickled Dilly Green Beans 59

Fresh Apple Cake 60

Spring Pea Vichyssoise with Vegetable Confetti 62

Vidalia Onion Canapés. 63

Lavender Blue Dilly Dilly Green Bean Salad 64

Apple Salad with Sherry & Honey Vinaigrette 65

Oven-Roasted Sweet Potato Tailgate Salad 66
Lowcountry Seafood Gumbo 67
Southern Smothered Corn Chowder 69
Cornmeal-Crusted Fried Okra 70
Fall Harvest Bisque 73
Fresh Peach Macaroon Tarts. 74
Sullivan's Smothered Corn with Frizzled Bacon. 75

SUNDAY BRUNCH AT SULLIVAN'S

Dana Sue's Almond-Filled Croissants 79
Classic Cream Scones 81
Frosted Café Royale 82
Lemon & Poppy Seed Scones. 83
Cranberry-Orange Scones with Orange Glaze 84
Gingerbread Scones. 86
Cranberry-Orange Butter 87
Macaroon Muffins with Dates & Pecans. 88
Lowcountry Crab Hash. 89
Microwave Lemon Curd 90
Stuffed French Toast with Glazed Strawberries 91
Spicy Shrimp & Sausage with Country Ham Cream-Style Gravy
over Creamy Yellow Grits 92
Chicken Salad with Dijon-Dill Dressing & Toasted Almonds 94
Pineapple Chicken Salad 95
Barbecue Salad with Tangy Coleslaw 96
Sullivan's Crab Cakes 97
Sherry Hollandaise Sauce 98
Carolina Rémoulade Sauce. 99
Country Ham & Grits Quiche with Red-Eye Gravy 100
Crustless Broccoli & Three-Cheese Quiche 102
Caramelized Onion & Bacon Quiche 103
Petite Dilly Biscuits 104
Sweet Potato Biscuits. 105
Whipping Cream Drop Biscuits 106
Strawberry Preserves with Rose Geranium & Vanilla Essence. 107
Peach Cobbler Jam. 108
Jingle Bell Candied Cranberries. 109
Southern Christmas Ambrosia 110
Uptown Down-South Cheese Grits. 111

MAMA CRUZ'S RECIPE FILE

Dulce De Leche Cheesecake Bars 115

Chicken Enchilada Casserole with Speedy Mole Sauce 116

Jacked-Up Tex-Mex Macaroni & Cheese 118

Pico de Gallo 119

Smoky Pork-Filled Tamales 120

Southern Seafood Paella 122

Black Bean Chili 124

Roasted Corn & Mixed Bean Salsa 126

Tex-Mex Appetizer Cheesecake 127

Tres Leches Cake 128

CHEF ERIK'S DECADENT DESSERTS

Pluff Mud Fudgy Bottom Peanut Butter Icebox Pie 133

Southern Supreme Red Velvet Cake 134

Buttermilk-Glazed Carrot Cake with Orange Cream Cheese Frosting 136

Coconut Cream Tart in Pecan Shortbread Crust 138

Southern Cream Cheese Pound Cake 139

Cinnamon Roll Bread Pudding with Whipped Vanilla Bean Crème 140

Baked Apple Bread Pudding with Cinnamon Ice Cream & Caramel Sauce . . 141

Pumpkin Cake Roll 142

Chocolate Sugarplum Truffles 145

Deep-Dish Apple Pie with Crunchy Crumb Topping 146

Valentine's Special Decadence Cake (flourless chocolate cake) 148

Warm Walnut Brownie à la Mode with Hot Fudge Sauce 151

Candied Orange Peel 152

Southern Pecan Toffee 154

Chocolate Amaretto Cake (no sugar added) 155

THE CORNER SPA'S LOW-CAL HEALTHY SELECTIONS

Corner Spa Tortilla Soup (low-fat) 159

Summer Gazpacho 160

Vidalia Onion Vinaigrette (fat-free) 161

Corner Spa Cream of Carrot Soup (low-fat) 162

Cucumber Cooler 165

Southern Legacy Apple & Mint Spritzer (no sugar added) 166

Fuzzy Navel Smoothie 167

Chunky Apple Bran Muffins (*low-fat*) 169
Almond Biscotti. 170
Chicken Caesar Salad Wraps 172
Mixed Salad with Strawberry & Basil Vinaigrette. 173
Balsamic Vinaigrette (*fat-free*). 174
Gold Nugget Chicken & Pasta Salad. 175

HOLIDAYS & GET-TOGETHERS

Christmas Festival Eggnog (*alcohol-free*). 179
Poinsettia Punch 180
Golden Wassail (*alcohol-free*) 181
White Sangria. 182
Front Porch Sippin' Lemonade 183
Iced Almond-Lemonade Tea 184
Hot Cocoa 187
Homemade Marshmallows 188
Crabgrass 190
Mulled Wine Punch. 191
Spicy Pickled Shrimp 192
Orange & Toasted Pecan Appetizer Torte. 193
Amaretto & Pecan Baked Brie. 194
Port Wine & Apple Cheddar Spread 195
Rolled Stuffed Turkey Breast. 196
Honey-Kissed Hot Apple Cider with Ginger 197
Hoppin' John New Year's Salad 198
Pepperoni Chips 198
Chili Bacon Sticks 199
Backyard Lowcountry Seafood Boil. 200
Pecan-Crusted Chicken Breasts with Pralines & Cream Sauce. 202
Praline Liqueur. 204
Pastel Butter Mints 205
Erik's Grilled Cheese Panini with Pecan-Pesto Mayo
& Spicy Tomato Jam. 206
Chocolate Cloud Cookies. 209
Sunburst Lemon Bars 210
Fall Festival Munch Mix. 212
Old-Fashioned Molasses Cookies. 213

Conversion Charts 214
About the Authors 217
Index 219

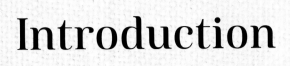

Introduction

Throughout the Sweet Magnolias books—all eleven of them—and in the television version currently on Netflix, food plays an important role. Southern food. Grits and gravy. Fried chicken. Red velvet cake. Peach cobbler. Bread pudding. Oh, my! I can gain ten pounds just writing about these things. As for eating them, it's best I not go there, at least on a regular basis. Moderation, that's the key. I try to remember that in real life, if not in my fictional world of Serenity, South Carolina.

The talk of food is particularly prominent in *A Slice of Heaven*, Dana Sue's story centered around Sullivan's—her regional success story, a restaurant known for putting a new spin on traditional Southern dishes. But food—and drink—also comes into play at the infamous margarita nights held by the group of old friends who call themselves the Sweet Magnolias, at the café in The Corner Spa, where less caloric offerings are available, and in the many backyard get-togethers of the Sweet Magnolias and their families. These Southern gals are, you see—like the friends you have in your community or neighborhood—always ready to share a meal and have some fun. Viewers get a feel for that in every episode of the TV series when

JoAnna Garcia Swisher (Maddie), Brooke Elliott (Dana Sue) and Heather Headley (Helen) gather together to "pour it out" in their version of the books' (and my own personal) margarita nights.

As for myself, I have an interesting relationship with food: I love to eat! A little too much, perhaps. I also love to write about food. I guess I must be good at inventing things, because the funny thing is, I've never really considered myself much of a cook.

While growing up, I demonstrated little interest in learning to cook, but by the time I was in my early teens, I was the default cook in my family. My working mother hated to cook. My dad enjoyed it, but he also worked. If I expected dinner at a reasonable hour, I had to make it, so I set out to learn a few basics. I managed to get food on the table most of the time. At least until the night my parents arrived home to find me standing in the yard in tears and cradling my hand, which I'd managed to sear with hot grease, probably while attempting to fry chicken. That gave my mother pause. In the end, though, I kept cooking. Nothing fancy, mind you. No baking pies or cakes. No exotic, complicated dishes. Just get-it-over-with meals that were edible.

Once I was out and on my own, my repertoire expanded. I was, after all, trying to impress a date from time to time. I recall the first Thanksgiving dinner I made for friends. I had to call my dad, the grand master of the Thanksgiving meal in our household, to figure out what on earth I was supposed to do with the turkey. He also coached me through our family's traditional dressing and how to perfect our favorite sweet potatoes with marshmallows.

These days I do more writing about cooking than actual cooking, but I still like to get into the kitchen and try to impress some of my friends. It seems that a lot of them have taken cooking classes or belong to some gourmet club that hosts fancy monthly dinner parties. I'm traumatized every time I invite them to dinner. My proudest moment came a few days after I'd grilled grouper and served it with a mango-papaya chutney I'd made from scratch. A friend reported having a similar dish at a fancy restaurant we all love and said, "Yours was better!" So, apparently, I do have my moments of culinary triumph.

Then one day I was busy writing away—no doubt creating dishes on the page but not in the kitchen—when my publisher suggested that it might be nice to have a cookbook reflecting all the many occasions on which food plays a comforting or celebratory role for the Sweet Magnolias. While I was still trying to wrap my mind around that outrageous thought, along came an out-of-the-blue email from a reader named Teddi Wohlford.

Teddi said she loved the Sweet Magnolias books, then added that she identified particularly with Dana Sue because she, too, is a Southern chef. She was also, as it turned out, the answer to my prayers. Teddi cooks! She caters! She's published a couple of Southern cookbooks of her own! Well, you can see how this might be a match made in publishing heaven.

Since the Sweet Magnolias series began, many of you have asked about recipes for some of the dishes mentioned. Here they are, along with many, many more created by Teddi, who (like Dana Sue) has put a new spin on many traditional Southern dishes and kicked 'em up a notch. This cookbook was written based on the books—the TV series follows its own path, which may differ at times—but I hope you will enjoy it nonetheless. I have worked my way through these incredible recipes and developed a whole new relationship with my Fitbit along the way. But trust me, it's been worth it. I hope you enjoy them as much as I do!

Sherryl Woods

Sweet Magnolias
Margarita Nights

Hey, y'all. I'm Dana Sue Sullivan, one of the three original Sweet Magnolias, and I'll be your guide through these pages. I'll tell you a little about myself, a lot about Serenity, South Carolina, and a few secrets I'm probably supposed to be keeping to myself.

I'd like to believe the task was turned over to me because, as the owner of Sullivan's, I'm the best cook, but the truth is everyone else in Serenity is so darn busy. Or suddenly claims to be. You know how it goes.

Here's a little background on the Sweet Magnolias to start. Three of us—Helen Decatur-Whitney, Maddie Maddox and I—have been best friends since we met on the playground at Serenity Elementary School, which at the time was the only elementary school in town. Now there are two. That's how small Serenity is, which can be both a blessing and a curse. Neighbors around here sure do have a way of getting in your business. I think they like to look at it as part of the small-town Southern charm, though personally I'm a lot fonder of some of our other traditions.

At any rate, I won't say just how long ago it was when the three of us started calling ourselves the Sweet Magnolias, but I spotted my first gray hair the other day. That alone was almost traumatic enough to call for a margarita night.

You see, that's what margarita nights are all about: friends getting together to support one another in a crisis, no matter how large or small. Helen, Maddie and I have faced our share of crises over the years, I can tell you that. Divorces, controversy, serious problems with our kids. We sometimes joke that Helen became a lawyer just because she knew we'd all eventually land in so much hot water!

Whenever there's trouble for any one of us—or for any of the many women we've welcomed into the fold in recent years—the first thing we do is call for a margarita night. It used to be that these get-togethers were impromptu, but now that there are so many of us and our schedules are so crazy, we have to plan for them. Either way, planned or spontaneous, I'm not sure what we'd do without these occasions when we can let off steam.

It's not about Helen's Lethal Margaritas, not really. Nor is it about my Killer Guacamole, though it is to die for, if I do say so myself. It's about friends supporting friends through tough times. It's about finding laughter through the tears, about giving advice—whether it's wanted or not. We can even manage to keep our opinions to ourselves from time to time if that's requested, though I assure you, it's not our first choice.

Now that some of us are getting a little older (my daughter and her friends are now Sweet Magnolias, for goodness' sake, as is Helen's mother, Flo, much to Helen's dismay), we've added some more substantial food to these gatherings. Those C'mon, Baby, Light My Fire Chicken Wings are just one of the recent additions. You'll find more ideas here for fleshing out a menu that can even be put together at a moment's notice.

But, like I said, it's not about the drinks. Or the food. Those are incidental to the camaraderie. All it really takes to achieve the perfect margarita night is getting a group of women together to make the burden of your troubles a little lighter. No matter what you're facing, don't you find it's always a little easier when you're surrounded by friends? I sure do.

Helen's Lethal Margaritas

SERVES 4

1 (6-ounce) can frozen limeade concentrate

¾ cup tequila

¼ cup Triple Sec or Grand Marnier

2 tablespoons agave nectar or honey

Okay, y'all, it doesn't get much easier than this—and sooo delish!

Fill the container of a blender with 4 cups of ice. Add all ingredients. Secure lid on blender, and blend until smooth. Pour into 4 salt-rimmed margarita glasses, or simply pass straws to your best friends and let everyone gather around.

STRAWBERRY MARGARITAS—substitute 12 ounces of frozen strawberries for 2 cups of the ice in the recipe.

MANGO MARGARITAS (Dana Sue's favorite!)—substitute 12 ounces of frozen mango chunks for 2 cups of the ice in the recipe.

> **NOTE:** Agave nectar comes from the same plant that tequila is made from. You can find it in most grocery stores today or in health food or nutrition stores. It makes a really authentic margarita!

Dana Sue's Killer Chunky Guacamole

MAKES 3½–4 CUPS, depending on the size of the avocados.

3 ripe avocados

Zest and juice of 1 lime

½ cup diced ripe (firm) tomato

⅓ cup finely diced purple onion

¼ cup minced fresh cilantro

4 garlic cloves, minced

2 jalapeño peppers

Sea salt to taste

1 Using a sharp knife, cut avocados in half, lengthwise. Remove and reserve pit from each avocado. Carefully scoop out avocado from the peel, then dice into small to medium chunks.

2 Combine avocado with lime zest and juice in a medium mixing bowl. Stir gently.

3 Add tomato, onion, cilantro and garlic.

4 As far as the jalapeño goes, you decide whether you want this guacamole fiery hot, mild or somewhere in between. For the hot stuff, leave in all the seeds and ribs of the peppers. For the less brave, remove all the seeds. And for wimps, you'll want to remove all the seeds *and* the ribs of the peppers.

5 Season to taste with sea salt. Stir gently to blend, trying not to mash the avocado.

6 Place the avocado pits in the bowl with the guacamole, then cover the bowl tightly with plastic food wrap. Refrigerate up to 1 day before serving.

To Serve

Remove the pits. Serve with fresh, crisp tortilla chips and your favorite salsa. Of course, margaritas are a must!

Magnolia Blossom Cocktail

MAKES 1 COCKTAIL

1 jigger vanilla vodka

1 jigger half-and-half

2 tablespoons vanilla-infused simple syrup

¼ teaspoon orange flower water

4–6 ounces chilled lemon-lime soda

½ teaspoon grated lemon zest

In a tall glass filled with ice, add first 4 ingredients. Add lemon-lime soda to near top of glass. Stir gently. Add grated lemon zest on top of cocktail.

> **NOTE:** Make your own simple syrup for cocktails rather than purchasing it at a gourmet market. Simply combine 1 cup water and 1 cup granulated sugar in a small saucepan. Bring to a boil, stirring to dissolve the sugar. Remove from heat, and let cool to room temperature. (Stir in 1 teaspoon vanilla for a vanilla-infused simple syrup.) Store any unused simple syrup in the refrigerator for use within a week or so. You can also freeze the syrup to extend the life for up to 2 months.

Snow Cream Martinis

SERVES 6

1½ cups vanilla vodka

½ cup white chocolate liqueur

½ cup sweetened condensed milk

3 cups chipped ice or small ice cubes

Combine all ingredients in a blender. Process until almost smooth.

> **NOTE:** This festive cocktail tastes like a winter wonderland!

Mint Juleps

MAKES 6 CUPS

3 loosely packed cups washed fresh mint leaves

4 cups boiling water

¾ cup sugar

2 cups Maker's Mark whiskey

GARNISH (OPTIONAL)

Mint sprigs

1 Fill a large glass bowl with mint leaves. Reserve a few for garnish.

2 Pour boiling water over the mint. Cover with plastic wrap, and let steep until mixture reaches room temperature. Strain mint liquid, and discard leaves.

3 Add sugar to mint liquid, and stir to dissolve. Add whiskey.

4 Bottle as desired, then cork or seal bottles.

5 Refrigerate up to 6 months. Serve over crushed ice with a sprig of mint for garnish.

> **NOTE FROM DANA SUE:** I admit that I miss the (time-consuming) ceremony and cherished tradition of making individual mint juleps—crushing the mint, stirring the sugar until it dissolves, adding bourbon, then pouring over crushed ice—but I adore the ease of this recipe version! I almost always have the mixture on hand during the hot summer.

Citrus Bourbon Slushy

MAKES ALMOST 1 GALLON

8 cups water, divided

1 family-size tea bag
or 4 regular-size tea bags

1 packed cup light brown sugar

1 (12-ounce) can frozen orange juice
concentrate, thawed

1 (12-ounce) can frozen lemonade
concentrate, thawed

1 (6-ounce) can frozen limeade
concentrate, thawed

2 cups bourbon

1 Bring 2 cups water to a boil. Add tea bag(s). Let steep 5 minutes only.
Lift tea bag(s) from water after steeping, then discard.

2 Add brown sugar. Stir to dissolve.

3 Add remaining ingredients, and stir to blend.

4 Cover, and freeze 2–4 hours until slushy, stirring several times with
a fork while freezing.

> **NOTE:** This drink is almost as refreshing served over crushed ice
> instead of freezing. Dilute with lemon-lime or club soda if you
> prefer a less potent cocktail.

Fire & Ice Pickles

MAKES 4 PINTS

2 (32-ounce) jars nonrefrigerated pickle slices

4 cups granulated sugar

2 tablespoons Tabasco sauce

1 teaspoon crushed red pepper flakes

4 minced garlic cloves

1 Combine all ingredients, and mix well.

2 Cover, and let stand at room temperature 3–4 hours, stirring occasionally.

3 Divide into 4 (1-pint) canning jars. Seal tightly.

4 Refrigerate up to 1 month.

> **NOTE:** Best if made at least 1 week before eating to allow flavors to develop.

C'mon, Baby, Light My Fire Chicken Wings

SERVES 4–12 (you know what I mean!)

WINGS

30 chicken wings

1 envelope dry ranch dressing mix

1 cup flour

1 quart canola or vegetable oil

SAUCE

½ cup butter

3 packed tablespoons light brown sugar

½ cup mild hot sauce, such as Texas Pete Hot Sauce or Frank's RedHot Sauce

2 tablespoons apple cider vinegar

½ teaspoon garlic powder

½ teaspoon crushed red pepper flakes

Wings

1 Snip off wing tips from chicken wings, then cut wings into two sections (at the joint). Blot chicken wings dry using paper towels.

2 Place ranch dressing mix and flour in a zip-top gallon-size bag. Shake to blend.

3 Add wings (10 at a time) to bag. Seal shut, shake to coat lightly. Place coated wings on a plastic-lined baking sheet.

4 Repeat with remaining wings.

5 Refrigerate at least 30 minutes, or up to 1 day before frying.

6 When ready to fry, heat oil in deep fryer or Dutch oven until temperature reaches 375°F.

7 Fry wings in batches, cooking each batch 8–10 minutes.

8 Transfer wings from fryer to a plate lined with paper towels.

9 Repeat with remaining wings.

10 Place cooked wings in large bowl or pan, covering loosely with foil while preparing more. Make the sauce while the wings are cooking.

Sauce

In a small saucepan, melt the butter and brown sugar. When brown sugar has dissolved, whisk in the hot sauce and vinegar. Add remaining ingredients, and whisk until well blended.

To Serve

When all wings are fried, drizzle with sauce. Stir to coat well. The longer the wings sit in the sauce, the hotter they get. (For milder wings, remove from sauce after 15 minutes.)

> **NOTE:** This Sweet Magnolia recipe will remind you of buffalo wings, but down South, we gotta make it just a little something special. Gild the magnolia by serving with our blue cheese dressing (see page 13) and some celery sticks—to help cut the heat!

Cheddar Blossoms

MAKES ABOUT 80

2 cups (8 ounces) grated sharp cheddar cheese, room temperature

½ cup butter, room temperature

1¼ cups all-purpose flour

½ teaspoon sea salt

¼–½ teaspoon ground cayenne pepper (you decide!)

Poppy seeds

1 Preheat oven to 350°F.

2 Combine cheddar and butter in a medium mixing bowl. Blend well.

3 Whisk together flour, salt and cayenne pepper. Add to cheese and butter mixture. Blend well.

4 Fill the barrel of a cookie press with dough. Choose the five-petal flower disc, and secure onto the end of the cookie press.

5 Press cheddar blossoms onto ungreased cookie sheets, spacing 1" apart. (If dough is too firm, it will not press out easily. Microwave the dough briefly to soften, if necessary.)

6 Sprinkle some poppy seeds in the center of each blossom.

7 Bake 1 pan at a time in center of oven 20–25 minutes, until golden brown.

8 Immediately remove cheddar blossoms from cookie sheet, and transfer to cooling rack to cool completely.

9 Store in an airtight container at room temperature up to 2 weeks. Alternately, cover tightly, and freeze up to 4 months.

> **NOTE:** No Southern affair (whether plain or fancy) would be complete without cheese straws. This is the Sweet Magnolia version of cheese straws—making them just a bit more special with the addition of poppy seeds in the center of each darling little blossom. These are a yummy treat and greatly enjoyed at any cocktail buffet, wedding reception or simply with a glass of red wine.

Blue Cheese Dressing
with Cognac

MAKES 3 CUPS

1½ cups mayonnaise

1 cup heavy whipping cream

½ cup white wine vinegar

2 tablespoons cognac

4 ounces blue cheese crumbles, divided

Sea salt and freshly ground black pepper to taste

In a blender or food processor, combine first four ingredients with half of the blue cheese crumbles. Blend until smooth. Stir in remaining blue cheese, and season with salt and pepper. Cover, and refrigerate up to 1 month.

> **NOTE:** This drop-dead fabulous blue cheese dressing is a favorite of Sullivan's Restaurant patrons. On Margarita Nights, you can find the Sweet Magnolias feasting on chicken wings and celery sticks— being dunked first in this dressing.

Sullivan's Restaurant Specialties of the House

I'd like to say that Sullivan's was always my dream, but the truth is until my husband, Ronnie, and I split up, I hadn't put much thought into opening up my own restaurant. I was content to cook for anyone who'd hire me, though I have to say that most of the menu offerings at Serenity's mom-and-pop places didn't present much of a challenge. This has always been a fried chicken, potato salad and greens kind of town.

Now, as a born and bred South Carolinian, I like Southern cooking as much as anyone, but I just can't seem to keep myself from putting a little spin on the traditional dishes from time to time. I'd accumulated an entire file box of recipes over time, trying them out on Ronnie and my daughter, Annie, and the Sweet Magnolias every chance I got.

When I found out Ronnie had cheated on me—and about two seconds after I'd chased him off with a cast-iron skillet—I decided the time had come to do something exciting and challenging just for me. With encouragement from my best pals, Maddie and Helen, I put together the business plan for Sullivan's, a restaurant dedicated to putting some zip into regional specialties. Though I'm real proud of our fancy decor, the perfectly pressed linen tablecloths and napkins I insisted on and the painting by our world-renowned local botanical artist Paula Vreeland (Maddie's mom) in our foyer, it's the food that brings customers from all over the state.

Yes, that's right. They come from all over. Oh, I had plenty of doubters, folks around here who said I'd never make a success of an upscale restaurant without being in Charleston or Columbia. But guess what? I proved them wrong. The glowing reviews started coming in from the big newspapers and regional magazines—and so did the customers.

By the time Ronnie and I reconciled, I was a whole lot stronger than I'd been when we first fell in love way back in high school—and a successful restaurant owner to boot! By then I didn't need a man in my life, but the pitiful truth is I sure did want this particular man. You know how that goes. Some things just never change. When the right man comes along, it's hard to get him out of your system, even after he's made a mistake the size of Ronnie's. Sometimes you just have to take a leap of faith that the apologies and the commitment are sincere.

Now I wouldn't share my trade secrets with just anyone, but folks keep asking about certain dishes, like my catfish with its spicy cornmeal coating or the peachy grilled chicken in a spicy peanut sauce. See what I mean? These are not the same old same old.

There are a lot more recipes here, straight off the Sullivan's menu. Pretty soon you'll be just like me, taking something ordinary, adding a dash of this and a teaspoonful of that and kicking all your cooking up a notch. But if you get any ideas about opening your own restaurant, promise you'll steer clear of Serenity. There's only room for one gourmet restaurant in this town, and Sullivan's has filled that niche. At least I like to think it has.

Toasted Pecan & Red Pepper Jam

8 (½ pint) canning jars, lids and screw-on bands

2 cups (about 8 ounces) pecan halves

1 green bell pepper, seeded, finely chopped

1 red bell pepper, seeded, finely chopped

6–8 jalapeño peppers, seeded (if desired), finely chopped

1½ cups apple cider vinegar

1 tablespoon butter

6½ cups sugar

1 (3-ounce) pouch liquid fruit pectin

1 Place jars, lids and bands in a large pot. Fill with hot water. Bring to a boil over high heat, and boil at least 5 minutes.

2 Scatter pecan halves on a rimmed baking sheet. Bake at 350°F about 10 minutes, just until nuts begin to smell toasted. Remove from oven, and let cool. Using a serrated knife, coarsely chop pecans.

3 Place peppers in a 1½–2 gallon saucepan or Dutch oven. Add vinegar and butter. Stir in sugar and pecans. Cook mixture over high heat, stirring often. Bring mixture to a full rolling boil that cannot be stirred down.

4 Stir in pectin. Return to a boil, and boil exactly 1 minute, stirring constantly. Remove from heat. Skim off any foam with a metal spoon.

5 Ladle immediately into prepared jars, filling to within ¼" of tops. Wipe jar rims clean. Cover with two-piece lids. Screw bands securely.

6 Place jars on elevated rack in canner. Lower rack into canner. Water must cover jars by 1–2". Add boiling water, if necessary.

7 Cover, and bring water to a gentle boil. Process 10 minutes in boiling water bath.

8 Remove jars, place upright on towel to cool 30 minutes, then turn jars upside down.

9 Alternate jars upright, then upside down for the first 2 hours of cooling to help suspend pecans and peppers in jam. Cool completely.

10 After jars cool, check seals by pressing middle of lids with finger. If lid springs back, lid is not sealed, and refrigeration is necessary. Properly sealed jars can be stored at room temperature up to 2 years.

NOTE: Enjoy with grilled poultry, pork or most seafood. Super yummy served with cream cheese and crackers for a speedy appetizer. Also makes a great bread-and-butter gift.

Garlic Toast Rounds

MAKES ABOUT 60 PIECES

1 French baguette, cut into ¼" slices

½ cup extra virgin olive oil

Garlic & herb seasoning

1 Preheat oven to 300°F.

2 Brush one side of each piece of bread with olive oil. Lightly sprinkle with garlic & herb seasoning.

3 Bake 30–40 minutes, until rounds are golden and completely dried out.

4 Remove from oven, and transfer to cooling rack. Allow to cool thoroughly before storing airtight up to 2 weeks.

> **NOTE:** Serve these delicious petite toasts with savory dips and fondues as well as alongside salads and soups.

Bacon & Swiss Appetizer Cheesecake

SERVES 16–20

CRUST

1½ cups finely crushed Ritz crackers

¼ cup melted butter

FILLING

2 (8-ounce) packages cream cheese, softened

2 eggs

2 cups grated Swiss cheese

10 slices bacon, cooked, crumbled

½ teaspoon dried basil

¼ teaspoon dried marjoram

¼ teaspoon dried thyme

⅛ teaspoon freshly grated nutmeg

Salt and pepper to taste

TOPPING

1 cup sour cream

3 slices bacon, cooked, crumbled

¼ cup chopped green onions

SERVE WITH:

Crackers

Toast rounds or points

Crust

1 Preheat oven to 325°F.

2 Stir together cracker crumbs and butter.

3 Press into the bottom of a 9" springform pan.

4 Bake 15 minutes. While crust is baking, prepare filling.

Filling

1 Combine all ingredients, and beat well with an electric mixer.

2 Spread filling over baked crust.

3 Bake 30 minutes.

4 Remove from oven, and place on cooling rack.

Topping

While the cheesecake is still warm, top with sour cream, and spread evenly over entire surface. Allow it to come to room temperature. Top with crumbled bacon and green onions. Cover, and refrigerate until ready to serve (within 3 days).

To Serve

Loosen cheesecake from pan by running a knife around the edge, then release spring, and remove cheesecake along with the bottom of the pan from the walls. Serve in small wedges with an assortment of crackers or homemade toast rounds or points.

Shrimp, Crab & Swiss Appetizer Cheesecake

SERVES 16

1½ cups finely crushed Ritz crackers

2 cups (8 ounces) grated Swiss cheese, divided

¼ cup butter, melted

3 (8-ounce) packages cream cheese, softened

3 large eggs

1 tablespoon OLD BAY Seasoning

½ teaspoon cayenne pepper

8 ounces fresh lump crabmeat, picked through

8 ounces cooked, squeezed dry salad-size shrimp

8 ounces sour cream, room temperature

1 chopped bunch green onions

Crust

1 Preheat oven to 350°F.

2 Spray the inside of a 9" springform pan completely with cooking spray.

3 Combine cracker crumbs, 2 ounces (½ cup) of the grated Swiss and melted butter. Press firmly in bottom of prepared pan.

4 Bake 15 minutes. While crust is baking, prepare filling.

Filling

1 Combine cream cheese, eggs, OLD BAY Seasoning and cayenne. Beat until smooth.

2 Stir in crabmeat, shrimp and remaining 6 ounces of grated Swiss cheese.

3 Pour onto baked crust. Using a spatula, level filling.

4 Bake 45 minutes.

5 Let cool in pan on cooling rack 10 minutes. (You may need to run a thin knife around inside of pan if filling has stuck to pan.)

6 Release spring, and carefully remove springform wall from cheesecake.

7 Evenly spread sour cream over top of cheesecake. Cool to room temperature.

8 Sprinkle top with green onions. Cover, and refrigerate up to 2 days before serving.

Cheddar Corn Muffins

MAKES 12

2⅔ cups corn muffin mix
(see next recipe)*

1 (14½-ounce) can whole-kernel corn,
drained

6 ounces grated cheddar cheese

1 cup sour cream

2 eggs, beaten

1 Preheat oven to 400°F.

2 Grease a standard-size 12-cup muffin tin.

3 In a large mixing bowl, combine first 3 ingredients.

4 In a separate small bowl, blend together sour cream and eggs. Stir into dry mixture.

5 Divide batter among muffin cups. Let rest at room temperature 5–10 minutes.

6 Bake 18–20 minutes, until tester inserted in center comes out clean, and center of muffin springs back when touched.

7 Let muffins cool in pan 2–3 minutes. Remove from pan, and transfer to cooling rack. Serve warm.

* If you choose not to make your own corn muffin mix, you can use 2 (8½-ounce) packages of store-bought corn muffin mix.

NOTE: These muffins are such a breeze to make and absolutely delicious served with almost any soup, stew or chili.

Corn Muffin Mix

MAKES ABOUT 10 CUPS

4¾ cups all-purpose flour

4 cups yellow cornmeal

1 cup sugar

4 tablespoons baking powder

2 tablespoons salt

1 cup all-vegetable shortening

Combine all ingredients, and blend well using either a food processor or handheld pastry blender. Freeze in an airtight freezer bag for use within 6 months.

Navy Bean Soup

SERVES 6–8

1 pound dried navy beans

8 cups chicken broth or stock

1 (28-ounce) can diced tomatoes

2 cups medium-diced yellow onions

8 ounces deli ham, cubed small

1 cup thinly sliced celery

2 bay leaves

2 tablespoons Worcestershire sauce

1 tablespoon soy sauce

1 tablespoon minced garlic

¼ teaspoon freshly grated nutmeg

Salt and freshly ground black pepper to taste

GARNISH (OPTIONAL)

½ cup minced fresh parsley

1 Place dried beans in a colander, and flush with running water. Sort through beans, and remove any bits of debris.

2 Place rinsed beans in a Dutch oven. Fill pot with water, covering beans by several inches. Soak at least 8 hours.

3 Drain beans, and return to the pot. Add chicken broth and all remaining ingredients except for salt, pepper and parsley.

4 Bring soup to a boil, and boil gently 1 hour.

5 Reduce heat to simmer. Cover pot with lid, and simmer 3 hours, until beans are tender.

6 Season with salt and pepper. Garnish with parsley just before serving.

> **NOTE:** Pair this hearty and healthy soup with a piece of cornbread or a warm yeast roll and butter. A crisp garden salad is the ideal accompaniment.

Lowcountry She-Crab Soup

SERVES 6-8

1 cup finely diced Vidalia onion (or other sweet yellow onion)

1 cup finely diced celery

¾ cup (1½ sticks) butter

¾ cup all-purpose flour

6 cups chicken stock

2 (10-ounce) bottles clam juice

½ teaspoon ground mace

1 tablespoon OLD BAY Seasoning

1 teaspoon white pepper

2 cups heavy whipping cream

2 tablespoons dry sherry

2 tablespoons cognac (or brandy)

1 pound fresh lump crabmeat, picked through

1 tablespoon crab roe (optional)*

1 In a large saucepan or small Dutch oven, sauté onion and celery in butter over medium-high heat, cooking until vegetables are tender.

2 Add flour, and cook 2–3 minutes, stirring constantly.

3 While whisking, pour in chicken stock and clam juice. Season soup with mace, OLD BAY Seasoning and white pepper.

4 Lower heat to simmer, and cook at least 15 minutes.

5 Stir in cream, sherry and cognac. Heat through for about 5 minutes.

6 Add crabmeat and roe. Stir gently but thoroughly to blend—you don't want to break up that beautiful crabmeat.

* I get my crab roe from my trusted seafood purveyor because it's a hard-to-come-by item. You can make the soup without the crab roe (and it still tastes fabulous without it), but it wouldn't be she-crab soup. I've heard that if you're unable to find crab roe, you can substitute a finely chopped, hard-cooked egg.

Gullah Peanut & Sweet Potato Soup

SERVES 6–8

¼ cup butter

½ cup chopped onion

½ cup chopped celery

6 cups peeled, coarsely grated sweet potato (about 2 pounds)

8 cups chicken stock or broth

1 cup smooth peanut butter

Salt and freshly ground black pepper to taste

GARNISH (OPTIONAL)

Chopped roasted, salted peanuts

1 In a large soup pot, melt butter over medium heat. Add onion, celery and sweet potatoes. Sauté until onion and celery are soft but not browned, about 5 minutes.

2 Add stock or broth, and bring to a boil.

3 Reduce heat to low. Cover, and simmer until sweet potatoes are very tender, about 30 minutes.

4 Remove from heat, and let cool slightly.

5 Working in batches, puree in a blender or food processor.

6 Return to saucepan, and whisk in peanut butter until mixture is smooth and heated through; do not boil.

7 Season to taste with salt and pepper. Ladle into soup bowls, and garnish with chopped peanuts.

Sherried Mushroom Soup

SERVES 6

2 tablespoons butter

1 medium onion

1 pound cleaned, sliced mushrooms

¼ cup minced fresh parsley

1 garlic clove, minced

1 tablespoon minced fresh thyme or 1 teaspoon dried

3 cups chicken broth or stock

4 cups half-and-half

2 cups heavy whipping cream

1 tablespoon sugar

1 teaspoon salt

¼ teaspoon freshly ground black pepper

3 tablespoons cornstarch

½ cup golden sherry

1 In a Dutch oven over medium-high heat, sauté first 6 ingredients until softened.

2 Add stock or broth, half-and-half and whipping cream. Bring to a boil over medium heat.

3 Reduce heat, and season with sugar, salt and pepper.

4 Dissolve cornstarch in sherry. Add to soup, stirring constantly until thickened.

> **NOTE:** Creamy, rich and delicious, this is an elegant soup. Drastically lower the fat and calories by using fat-free half-and-half or milk.

Baby Greens

with Pears, Blue Cheese & Toasted Walnut Vinaigrette

SERVES 6

1½ cups walnut halves

VINAIGRETTE

½ cup sherry vinegar or white wine vinegar

2 tablespoons orange marmalade

1 tablespoon Dijon mustard

1 tablespoon fresh thyme leaves or 1 teaspoon dried

1 cup canola or vegetable oil

½ cup walnut oil

Salt and freshly ground black pepper to taste

SALAD

12 cups mixed baby greens

½ red onion, sliced paper-thin

3 medium pears, quartered, cored, thinly sliced

4 ounces blue cheese crumbles

⅔ cup sweetened, dried cranberries (such as Craisins)

8 thin, crispy gingersnap cookies, broken into pieces

Preheat oven to 350°F. Place walnut halves on a baking sheet, and bake 10–12 minutes, just until nuts begin to smell toasty. Remove from oven, and let cool to room temperature. Using a serrated knife, coarsely chop walnuts.

Vinaigrette

1 In a blender or food processor, combine vinegar, marmalade, mustard and thyme.

2 With machine running, add oils through the top of the machine in a thin, steady stream.

3 Season to taste with salt and pepper.

4 Add ½ cup toasted walnut pieces. Process briefly.

Salad

On each of 6 salad plates (or 1 large salad platter), arrange the baby greens. Top the salad greens with the remaining 1 cup walnut halves, onion, pears, blue cheese, cranberries and gingersnaps. Drizzle with the vinaigrette.

> **NOTE:** This is one our favorite recipes for a tasty and elegant composed salad. All the flavors work so well together, and it's so pretty to serve!

Citrus Salmon

with Crunchy Crumb Topping

SERVES 6

6 boneless, skinless salmon fillets, about 6 ounces each

Salt and freshly ground black pepper to taste

MARINADE

¾ cup orange marmalade

¾ cup Worcestershire sauce for chicken

½ cup orange juice

Grated zest and juice of 1 lemon

Grated zest and juice of 1 lime

2 tablespoons coarse-grain Dijon mustard

2 tablespoons dried, minced onion

1 teaspoon ground ginger

CRUMB TOPPING

½ cup coarsely crushed gingersnap cookies

½ cup coarsely crushed croutons

Marinade

1 Combine all marinade ingredients in blender or food processor. Blend until almost smooth.

2 Arrange salmon in a single layer in a gallon-size zip-top plastic bag.

3 Pour ⅔ of the marinade over salmon. (The remaining marinade will be used as a finishing sauce.)

4 Refrigerate 8–24 hours, turning bag over several times.

Salmon

1 Remove salmon from marinade, and pat dry.

2 Sprinkle with salt and freshly ground black pepper.

3 Cook according to your preference, whether broiling, pan-searing in a skillet or grilling over hot coals.

4 Serve cooked salmon with remaining marinade drizzled over top.

Crumb Topping

Mix ingredients together. Sprinkle salmon liberally with crumb topping just before serving.

Sea Bass

with Vegetables & Herbs en Papillote

SERVES 6

6 pieces (16"×12") baking parchment

6 (8-ounce) pieces boned, skinned sea bass

Sea salt

Freshly ground black pepper

⅓ cup finely minced fresh tarragon or 2 tablespoons dried

2 medium yellow crookneck squash, very thinly sliced

2 medium zucchini squash, very thinly sliced

3 peeled medium carrots, cut into match sticks

3 peeled shallots, sliced paper-thin

1 pound asparagus (tough ends trimmed, discarded; spears cut in half)

4 ounces melted black truffle butter or ½ cup black truffle oil

SIDE (OPTIONAL)

Basmati or Carolina Gold Rice*

1 Preheat oven to 425°F.

2 Place a piece of sea bass in the center of each piece of baking parchment. Sprinkle each with sea salt, pepper and tarragon.

3 Divide all vegetables equally in layers on top of the fish. Sprinkle again with sea salt and pepper.

4 Drizzle the melted truffle butter (or oil) over the vegetables.

5 **ASSEMBLE THE PARCHMENT PACKETS:** Gather the two long sides of parchment to the center. Make a ½" fold, and roll down 2 or 3 times, creasing each fold to make a tight seal. Fold both sides of each end toward a center point, creasing to seal. Fold each end snuggly under the packet.

6 Place 3 packets on each of 2 rimmed, foil-lined baking sheets. Bake 20 minutes.

7 Remove from oven, and let stand 5 minutes before transferring packets to individual serving plates.

---

* Carolina Gold Rice, a long grain rice, is an heirloom grain—a trendy ingredient first grown in the Lowcountry regions of South Carolina and Georgia in the late 1600s. Although it is a bit pricey, it is sought out by serious foodies for its delicious taste and enticing aroma. The gold in the name refers not to the color but to the economic stronghold that this lucrative staple maintained. It is available in grocery stores and gourmet kitchen shops in the Lowcountry of South Carolina and online at www.ansonmills.com.

8 Serve hot, letting each diner open own packet. Serve alongside hot, steamed basmati or Carolina Gold Rice to catch all those fabulous juices.

> **NOTE:** En papillote always refers to food prepared in packets. Baking parchment paper is traditional to the French method of preparation, although some people prefer to use aluminum foil. Each diner gets his or her own little package to be opened at the table just before dining. Who doesn't like having their own little present to open?!

Herb Cheese Spread

MAKES ABOUT 4 CUPS

2 (8-ounce) packages cream cheese, softened

1 cup butter, softened

2 garlic cloves, minced

1 teaspoon salt

½ teaspoon dried oregano

½ teaspoon dried basil

½ teaspoon dried dill weed

½ teaspoon dried lemon & pepper seasoning

½ teaspoon freshly ground black pepper

¼ teaspoon dried marjoram

¼ teaspoon dried thyme

1 tablespoon honey

In a medium mixing bowl, combine cream cheese and butter. Beat until light and fluffy. Add remaining ingredients, and blend well. Cover, and refrigerate up to 1 week, or freeze up to 2 months.

> **NOTE:** This creamy, dreamy appetizer spread is terrific! I just keep finding ways to use it. It's delicious spread on crackers and savory breads. It's also a perfect partner for hot pasta, a steamy baked potato or steamed vegetables. At Sullivan's Restaurant, we serve it with our bread baskets.

Bourbon & Brown Sugar Grilled Salmon

with Tropical Fruit Salsa

SERVES 4

4 (6-ounce) boned, skinned salmon fillets

MARINADE

¼ packed cup brown sugar

¼ cup soy sauce

¼ cup bourbon

Juice and zest of 1 orange

2 teaspoons minced fresh gingerroot

2 teaspoons minced fresh garlic

¼ teaspoon freshly ground black pepper

SALSA

1½ cups small-diced fresh golden (extra sweet) pineapple

1 peeled, small-diced kiwi

½ peeled, small-diced fresh mango

½ cup chopped green onions

1 fresh jalapeño pepper (seeds and ribs removed if milder heat is preferred)

¼ cup seasoned rice vinegar

1 tablespoon sugar

Salt and freshly ground black pepper to taste

GARNISH (OPTIONAL)

Chopped fresh cilantro

Marinade

Place salmon in a single layer in a glass container of suitable size or in a large zip-top food storage bag. Combine all marinade ingredients, and stir to dissolve sugar. Pour marinade over salmon fillets; cover, and refrigerate 1–8 hours, turning salmon several times. Prepare salsa while salmon is marinating.

Salsa

Combine all salsa ingredients, and toss gently but thoroughly. Cover, and leave at room temperature 1–8 hours before serving with the grilled salmon.

continued on next page

Salmon

1 After marinating, discard marinade, and pat salmon dry between paper towels.

2 Heat grill until very hot. Coat food rack with a nonstick grilling spray.

3 Place salmon fillets on food rack. Cook several minutes until cooked almost halfway through.

4 Carefully turn salmon over, and continue to cook just until desired degree of doneness. (Please, do not overcook!)

5 Transfer salmon to a serving platter, and serve topped with the room-temperature tropical fruit salsa. Garnish with cilantro.

Sweet & Tangy Tomato-Basil Vinaigrette

MAKES ABOUT 2½ CUPS

½ cup canned, crushed tomatoes

½ cup balsamic vinegar

¼ cup minced fresh basil leaves

½ cup freshly grated Parmesan cheese

2 tablespoons sugar

1 teaspoon salt

1 teaspoon freshly ground black pepper

1 cup extra-virgin olive oil

In a blender or food processor, blend together all ingredients except the olive oil. With the machine running, add the oil in a thin, steady stream.

NOTE: This recipe is best if made several hours or up to 3 days before serving. Serve over fresh salad greens or as a pasta salad dressing.

Shrimp Scampi Linguine

SERVES 6

1 cup freshly grated Parmesan cheese

1 pound linguine

SHRIMP

1 tablespoon cornstarch

¼ cup golden sherry

2 pounds large, raw, peeled, deveined shrimp

SAUCE

1 cup (2 sticks) butter

2 tablespoons Dijon mustard

1 teaspoon freshly grated lemon zest

1 tablespoon freshly squeezed lemon juice

¼ cup minced shallots

2 tablespoons minced fresh garlic

½ teaspoon crushed red pepper flakes

¼ cup minced fresh parsley

Shrimp

Preheat oven to 450°F. Place cornstarch in a medium mixing bowl. Whisk in sherry to dissolve cornstarch. Add shrimp, and stir to coat in cornstarch mixture. Let stand while preparing the sauce.

Sauce

1 In a small saucepan over medium-high heat, combine the first 7 ingredients. Stirring constantly, cook until butter melts and sauce develops. Remove from heat.

2 Stir in parsley. Arrange shrimp in a 13" × 9" × 2" baking pan or suitable casserole dish.

3 Pour sauce evenly over shrimp. Bake 10 minutes.

4 Remove from oven, and sprinkle with Parmesan cheese. Return to the oven for another 5 minutes.

5 Serve shrimp and sauce hot over freshly cooked linguine.

Panfried Catfish
with Spicy Cornmeal Coating

SERVES 4

1 cup vegetable or canola oil

CATFISH SOAK

2 cups buttermilk

½ teaspoon ground cayenne pepper

4 catfish fillets (6 ounces each)

CORNMEAL COATING

1 cup all-purpose flour

½ cup cornmeal

1 tablespoon Cajun and Creole seasoning

1 tablespoon garlic salt

1 tablespoon freshly grated lemon zest

½–1 teaspoon ground cayenne pepper (you decide!)

WET MIXTURE

3 eggs, beaten

3 tablespoons freshly squeezed lemon juice

Catfish Soak

In a medium mixing bowl, whisk together the buttermilk and cayenne pepper. Add catfish fillets, making sure each comes into contact with the soaking liquid. Refrigerate 4–12 hours. Remove catfish from soaking liquid, and pat dry between paper towels. Discard the soaking liquid.

Cornmeal Coating

Combine all ingredients in a gallon-size zip-top food storage bag. Secure shut, and shake to blend. Set aside.

Wet Mixture

In a shallow dish, whisk together the eggs and lemon juice.

Breading Procedure

Once you have dried off the catfish fillets after their buttermilk soak, you can proceed. The proper breading technique (for all frying) is a dry-wet-dry method. Dredge the catfish fillets, one at a time, into the spicy cornmeal coating, then the egg mixture, then back to the spicy cornmeal coating (dry, wet, dry).

Frying

1 Heat oil in a large skillet over medium-high heat to 370°F. (Check the temperature with a thermometer if you have one.) You will know when the oil is hot enough to fry if you drop a tiny bit of breading into the hot oil and it sizzles furiously. The oil should be hot but not smoking.

2 Carefully lower the catfish into the skillet, frying two fillets at a time. The thickness of the fillets determines the cooking time. Total frying time is approximately 7–8 minutes, turning once halfway through frying.

3 Remove from skillet, and let drain on wadded paper towels.

4 Repeat with remaining fillets.

> **NOTE:** Catfish can be quite strong tasting. The buttermilk soak helps lessen that strong (sometimes offensive) flavor. This buttermilk soak also works nicely with wild game and fowl. It also helps tenderize the meat some.

Pan-Seared Trout

with Browned Butter & Lemon Sauce

SERVES 4

SAUCE

½ cup butter

1 lemon

1 teaspoon coarsely ground
black pepper

TROUT

4 boneless rainbow trout fillets
(5–6 ounces each)

Salt and freshly ground black pepper

4 sprigs fresh rosemary

1 lemon, very thinly sliced

Sauce

1 Place butter in a small saucepan. Bring to a boil over medium heat. Continue to boil, stirring often, until nutty smelling and amber colored. Remove from heat.

2 Using a vegetable peeler, remove the lemon zest (colored part of the peel). Add lemon zest to the browned butter.

3 Juice the lemon, removing the seeds. Add lemon juice and pepper to the browned butter sauce. Cover sauce to keep warm while you prepare the fish.

4 Just before serving, remove the lemon zest, and discard.

Trout

1 Rinse trout fillets, and pat dry between paper towels, skin-side up. Season fish with salt and freshly ground black pepper.

2 Place a sprig of rosemary on each fillet. Place 2 slices of lemon on top of each rosemary sprig.

3 Heat a large skillet over medium-high heat. Spray pan lightly with nonstick cooking spray. Place 2 pieces of trout on skillet, flesh side up. Cook 3 minutes.

4 Carefully turn over with the lemon slices coming in direct contact with the skillet. Cook 2 minutes more.

5 Transfer to serving plates or platter, covering loosely with foil to keep warm while you prepare the other two trout fillets. Drizzle each serving with browned butter & lemon sauce.

Peachy Grilled Chicken

with Spicy Peanut Sauce

SERVES 12 as an appetizer or **6** as a main course.

CHICKEN

24 chicken tenders

1 (8-ounce) bottle teriyaki marinade

4 large, peeled fresh peaches, each cut into 12 wedges

24 bamboo skewers, soaked in water several hours

SAUCE

1½ cups hot water

½ cup crunchy peanut butter

1 teaspoon minced garlic

1 teaspoon ground ginger

Tabasco sauce to taste

Salt to taste

Chicken

1 Place chicken tenders in a zip-top bag. Add teriyaki marinade, and marinate according to package directions.

2 Remove tenders from marinade, and discard marinade. Pat chicken dry, using paper towels.

3 Secure one end of chicken tender onto pointed end of skewer. Add peach slice to the skewer, then bring the chicken tender around and over the peach slice, securing chicken again on the skewer. Slide another peach slice onto the skewer and wrap peach slice with the remainder of the chicken tender, securing end of chicken on skewer in "S" fashion.

4 Repeat process with remaining peaches and chicken. Prepare sauce before grilling chicken.

5 Heat grill.

Sauce

In a small saucepan, combine ingredients. Cook over medium heat, whisking constantly until thoroughly heated and thickened. Do not allow to boil. Keep warm while grilling chicken.

Grilling

Grill chicken over hot coals several minutes, turning once, until the chicken is no longer transparent. Serve hot or warm with peanut sauce.

Honey Grilled Pork Tenderloin
with Peach Salsa

SERVES 6

SALSA

3 cups peeled, chopped peaches

¼ cup minced fresh parsley

2 jalapeño peppers, seeded, finely chopped

2 tablespoons fresh lime juice

1 tablespoon sugar

1 tablespoon seasoned rice vinegar

1 teaspoon salt

PORK

2 pork tenderloins (1¼ pounds each)

⅓ cup soy sauce

½ teaspoon ground ginger

5 fresh garlic cloves, minced

2 tablespoons brown sugar

¼ cup honey

1 tablespoon dark sesame oil

3 tablespoons vegetable oil

Salsa

Combine all ingredients, stirring well. Cover, and refrigerate several hours or overnight. Bring to room temperature prior to serving over grilled pork tenderloin.

Pork

1 Butterfly tenderloins by making a lengthwise cut in each, cutting to within ¼" of other side. Place in a large zip-top bag.

2 Combine soy sauce, ginger and garlic in a small bowl. Pour over tenderloins. Seal bag, and refrigerate at least 3 hours (or overnight), turning occasionally.

3 Remove tenderloins, and discard marinade.

4 Combine brown sugar, honey and oils in a small saucepan. Cook over low heat, stirring constantly until the sugar dissolves. Set aside.

5 Heat grill; coals should be moderately hot. If using a gas grill, heat to medium.

6 Place tenderloins on a greased rack, and brush with the honey mixture. Grill 20 minutes, turning once and basting frequently, until meat thermometer inserted into the thickest portion registers 145–160°F. Slice, and serve immediately.

Roasted Spring Lamb
with Herbs & Madeira Sauce

SERVES 8–10

1 boneless leg of lamb

BREAD CRUMB–HERB–NUT MIXTURE

4½ cups fresh bread crumbs, divided

3 tablespoons minced fresh parsley or 1 tablespoon dried

3 tablespoons minced fresh chives or 1 tablespoon dried

1 tablespoon minced fresh thyme or 1 teaspoon dried

1 tablespoon minced fresh rosemary or 1 teaspoon dried

1 tablespoon minced fresh garlic

1 tablespoon salt

1 teaspoon freshly ground black pepper

½ cup coarsely chopped pistachio nuts

SAUCE

2 tablespoons butter

2 tablespoons flour

1 tablespoon tomato paste

1½ cups lamb or chicken stock

3 tablespoons Madeira

Salt and pepper to taste

Lamb

Preheat oven to 450°F. Cover roasting pan with foil. Split leg of lamb, and lay out flat to butterfly the lamb leg.

Bread Crumb–Herb–Nut Mixture

1 Combine all ingredients, and blend well. Reserve 1½ cups for coating.

2 Distribute remaining mixture evenly over butterflied lamb.

3 Roll, and secure by tying with kitchen twine at 2" intervals.

4 Coat exterior surface of lamb with remaining mixture.

Roasting

1 Place lamb on a rack in an open roasting pan. Roast in center of oven 30 minutes. Prepare Madeira sauce while roasting.

2 Reduce heat to 350°F. Roast 20 minutes per pound for medium doneness, until internal temperature registers 140°F on a meat thermometer. If you prefer your lamb more or less rare, adjust cooking times accordingly.

3 Remove lamb from oven, and let stand at room temperature 10 minutes.

4 Remove twine, and slice. Serve with sauce.

Sauce

In a medium saucepan, cook butter and flour together over medium heat until lightly browned. Whisk in tomato paste, stock and Madeira. Reduce heat to low, and simmer, stirring occasionally until sauce has thickened and reduced slightly. Season with salt and pepper.

"Oven-Fried" Chicken Tenders

SERVES 6

CHICKEN

2 pounds chicken tenders

¾ cup mayonnaise

CRACKER COATING

1½ cups finely crushed Ritz crackers

1 teaspoon garlic powder

1 teaspoon freshly ground black pepper

1 teaspoon paprika

Chicken

Preheat oven to 375°F. Line a jelly-roll pan or rimmed baking sheet with nonstick aluminum foil. Combine the chicken tenders with the mayonnaise. Stir to coat each piece.

Cracker Coating

Combine all ingredients in a gallon-size zip-top bag. Seal shut, and shake to blend together. Coat chicken tenders with crumb coating, working with 3 or 4 pieces at a time. Place on foil-lined baking pan, allowing a bit of space between each piece. Place in center of oven, and bake 25 minutes.

Garlic & Rosemary Roasted Pork Loin

with Sour Cream & Mushroom Sauce

SERVES 4–6

1 boneless pork loin

RUB

1 tablespoon vegetable oil

1 teaspoon minced garlic

½ teaspoon minced fresh rosemary

½ teaspoon salt

¼ teaspoon freshly ground
black pepper

SAUCE

Reserved, defatted pan drippings
from roasted pork loin

8 ounces thinly sliced fresh
mushrooms

3 tablespoons cornstarch

1 cup cold water

1 cup sour cream

Rub

Blend rub ingredients for each pound of pork loin. (**Example:** If the
pork weighs 3 pounds, triple the ingredients.) Score fatty side of
pork in a cross-hatch fashion ½–1" deep. Coat entire loin with rub.
Place in zip-top bag; refrigerate, and marinate up to 24 hours.

Roasting

Preheat oven to 325°F. Place marinated loin on rack in roasting pan.
Roast 1–1½ hours, or until a meat thermometer inserted into the center
of the roast registers 160°F. Transfer to serving platter, cover with foil,
and let stand 5–10 minutes before slicing and serving with sauce.

Sauce

1 Strain defatted drippings into a saucepan. Bring to a boil.

2 Add mushrooms, and cook 5 minutes.

3 Dissolve cornstarch in the cold water. While stirring, gradually
add to sauce. Cook and stir until thickened. Reduce heat to low.

4 Stir in sour cream. Heat through. Do not allow sauce to boil once
sour cream has been added.

Vegetarian Pasta Primavera
with Smoked Gouda Sauce

SERVES 6

1 pound dried pasta

SAUCE

1 medium onion, chopped

1 teaspoon minced garlic

½ cup butter

1 pound asparagus, trimmed, cut into 1" pieces

8 ounces sliced mixed mushrooms

8 cauliflower florets

1 medium zucchini, cut into thin slices

1 medium carrot, cut into thin slices

1 cup heavy whipping cream

½ cup chicken stock

3 tablespoons chopped fresh basil or 1 tablespoon dried

1 cup frozen young green peas, thawed

5 green onions, thinly sliced

Salt and pepper to taste

2 cups (8 ounces) grated smoked Gouda cheese

Sauce

1 In a large skillet over medium-high heat, sauté onions and garlic in butter until softened.

2 Add asparagus, mushrooms, cauliflower, zucchini and carrot. Sauté 3–5 minutes, stirring often.

3 Add cream, stock and basil. Bring to a gentle boil. Cook 3–5 minutes, stirring often, until liquid is slightly reduced.

4 Stir in peas and green onions. Cook 1 minute.

5 Season to taste with salt and pepper. Stir in grated cheese. Cook until cheese melts.

Pasta

While sauce is being prepared, cook pasta according to package directions. Drain thoroughly. Add to sauce, and toss gently. Garnish with additional basil, if desired.

Mixed Mushroom Risotto

SERVES 10

2 cups medium-diced Vidalia onion
(or other sweet yellow onion)

1 pound fresh mushrooms
(use a variety), thinly sliced

3 tablespoons olive oil

4 garlic cloves, minced

1 (16-ounce) package arborio
(Italian short-grain) rice

6 cups hot chicken broth

1 cup dry sherry

1 cup heavy whipping cream,
room temperature

1 cup freshly grated Parmesan
cheese, room temperature

Salt and pepper to taste

1 Sauté onions and mushrooms in hot oil in a Dutch oven over
medium heat until tender.

2 Stir in garlic, and sauté 1 minute more.

3 Add rice; stir to coat grains well.

4 Combine broth and sherry in a saucepan until very hot. Add a ladle
of hot broth to rice mixture, stirring constantly until almost all
liquid is absorbed. Continue to add broth, a ladle at a time, stirring
constantly until liquid is absorbed with each addition. This should
take approximately 25–30 minutes. Rice should be cooked until it
is al dente (still a tiny bit firm in the center of the grain).

5 Remove from heat. Add whipping cream and Parmesan cheese.
Stir to combine. Season as desired with salt and pepper. Serve
immediately—risotto waits for no one.

Three-Cheese Macaroni Casserole

SERVES 10–12

1 pound cooked elbow macaroni

2 cups (8 ounces) shredded smoked Gouda, divided

2 cups (8 ounces) shredded sharp cheddar, divided

4 large eggs, beaten

1½ cups milk

1 (8-ounce) package cream cheese, room temperature

1 teaspoon salt

½ teaspoon freshly ground black pepper

Dash cayenne pepper

1 Preheat oven to 350°F.

2 Generously grease a 3-quart casserole or baking dish. Distribute ½ the cooked macaroni in the bottom of the dish.

3 Combine shredded cheeses. Sprinkle 1½ cups cheese mixture over macaroni. Layer with remaining macaroni and an additional 1½ cups cheese mixture.

4 Blend remaining ingredients together. Pour over casserole. Cover tightly, and bake 45 minutes.

5 Remove cover, and top with remaining 1 cup cheese. Return to oven, and bake 10 minutes more.

Southern-Style Green Beans Amandine

with Frizzled Bacon & Smoked Almonds

SERVES 10–12

12 ounces thick-sliced pepper-coated bacon, cut into thin strips

3 pounds fresh or frozen whole green beans (if using frozen beans, thaw, rinse, and drain well)

Salt and freshly ground black pepper to taste

1 cup coarsely chopped smoked almonds

> **NOTE:** Gracious goodness, these are out-of-this-world good! Notice that I didn't say good for you. Save this dish for special occasions, when you're feeling indulgent or when you just want some great comfort food.

In a Dutch oven or very large skillet, cook bacon over medium-high heat until crisp. Remove with a slotted spoon. In reserved drippings, cook green beans until crisp and heated through, seasoning well with salt and pepper. Just before serving, stir in cooked bacon and almonds.

> **NOTE:** Smoked almonds aren't really smoked. They're roasted almonds coated in a smoky-seasoned salt. You'll find these delicious tidbits in the snack aisle of your grocery store, near the cocktail peanuts and other nuts.

Carolina Red Rice

SERVES 8

6 ounces thick-sliced, pepper-coated bacon, cut into thin strips

1 large onion, diced

2 cups converted rice

1 (28-ounce) can diced tomatoes, including juice

2 cups chicken stock or canned chicken broth

Salt and freshly ground black pepper to taste

1 In a large skillet over medium-high heat, cook bacon until crisp.

2 Add onion to skillet, and sauté until transparent.

3 Add rice, and stir to coat the grains. Add tomatoes and chicken stock. Bring to a boil.

4 Reduce heat to simmer. Cover, and cook until liquid is absorbed. Season with salt and pepper. Fluff with a fork before serving.

> **NOTE:** Why converted rice? Converted rice has been parboiled. When you cook with it, all the grains stay separate and never get mushy. Don't make the mistake of buying instant rice.

Sweet Potato Soufflé
with Pecan & Oat Streusel Topping

SERVES 8–10

SOUFFLÉ

2 (40-ounce) cans sweet potatoes (yams) packed in syrup, drained well

1 (14-ounce) can sweetened condensed milk

4 eggs, beaten

1 cup heavy whipping cream

1 tablespoon pure vanilla extract

Finely grated zest of 1 orange

½ teaspoon ground cinnamon

½ teaspoon freshly grated nutmeg

½ teaspoon salt

TOPPING

1¼ cups chopped pecans

1 packed cup light brown sugar

¾ cup old-fashioned oats

½ cup melted butter

¼ cup all-purpose flour

Soufflé

1 Preheat oven to 350°F.

2 Grease a 13" × 9" × 2" baking dish or suitable shallow casserole dish.

3 Using a food processor or potato masher, mash potatoes to desired degree of texture.

4 Add remaining soufflé ingredients, and blend well. Pour into prepared pan.

Topping

Combine all topping ingredients in a medium mixing bowl, stirring with a fork to blend. Evenly distribute over soufflé. Bake 45 minutes, then let stand 10 minutes before serving.

> **NOTE:** This recipe is intended to serve a crowd for your holiday meal gathering. If you want to halve the recipe, bake it in an 8" pan for 35 minutes.

Walnut-Crusted Potatoes

with Herbs

SERVES 6-8

CRUST

1 ½ cups French bread cubes

¾ cup walnuts

⅓ cup freshly grated Parmesan cheese

2 tablespoons butter, softened

POTATOES

3 pounds red potatoes

1 tablespoon minced fresh parsley

2 teaspoons minced fresh thyme
or 1 teaspoon dried

1½ teaspoons minced fresh sage
or ½ teaspoon dried

1 teaspoon salt

½ teaspoon freshly ground
black pepper

¼ cup olive oil

1 cup chicken broth

Crust

Combine ingredients in food processor. Blend well, and set aside.

Potatoes

1 Preheat oven to 375°F.

2 Grease a 13" × 9" × 2" baking pan.

3 Thinly slice unpeeled potatoes. Rinse, and drain.

4 Toss with herbs, salt and pepper. Distribute in prepared pan.

5 Drizzle with oil, and add chicken broth.

6 Cover tightly with foil. Bake 25–30 minutes.

7 Remove from oven, and increase oven temperature to 425°F.

8 Remove foil, and distribute crust over top. Bake uncovered
15–20 minutes, until top is golden brown.

Serenity
Farmers' Market

Every good cook knows there's nothing better than using fresh ingredients in a recipe. In summertime here in South Carolina, we're blessed with a bounty of fresh produce from local farmers. Believe you me, I take full advantage of that, whether I'm planning the specials for Sullivan's or just cooking for my family and friends.

Personally, I could be satisfied with one of those amazing beefsteak tomatoes straight from the garden every single day they're in season. Drizzle it with a little balsamic vinegar, add a slice of mozzarella, and you have a tasty salad that rises above the ordinary. But for most folks around here, variety is the spice of life. And why not, with fresh corn, greens, okra, squash, green beans, limas, zucchini and those sweet Vidalia onions available? And then there are the strawberries, blackberries, peaches and apples! Oh, my! Just wandering among the vendors at our local farmers' market is enough to get my mouth watering and my creative juices flowing. I always say that cooking is one part skill and one part inspiration.

Now, it used to be Southern cooks tossed their vegetables into some water, boiled the very life out of them, added enough butter to clog the arteries and then seasoned with more salt than the most lenient dietary recommendations call for. We've wised up in recent years. Now we've found all sorts of new ways to perk up veggies. I promise you, some of these are good enough they'll lure even the most suspicious youngster into gobbling them right up.

You're always free to eat that delicious corn straight off the cob at your backyard barbecue, but how about a hearty bowl of Southern smothered corn chowder as a change of pace? Or maybe a spring pea vichyssoise? Tired of your mama's potato salad? Take a sweet potato tailgate salad next time you head to the ball park.

As for all those delectable fruits that are available in summer, there's nothing quite like berries picked straight from the vine, still warm from sunshine, and popped straight into your mouth with all that sweetness bursting on your tongue. Or a ripe peach just off the tree, its juice dripping as you take that first bite. Heavenly.

But from time to time we all want to impress our guests with something a little fancier. Maybe it's a fruit cobbler or an all-American apple pie. Or just maybe you can earn their praise with an apple salad with a sherry and honey vinaigrette that's both tasty and healthy.

Now, if it were up to me, I'd have my own garden right outside my kitchen, but as a practical matter that's not likely to happen. I just don't have the time to do all that weeding and watering. So, if you can't find a patch of ground to grow your own produce, make sure you plan a visit to your local farmers' market as often as you can.

There are plenty of ideas right here in these pages for using whatever you find that's in season and grown locally. Or just take a walk through the market, draw in a deep breath, and let your imagination soar. With fresh ingredients straight from the garden, I can just about guarantee that whatever you fix for dinner will be extraordinary.

Pickled Green Tomatoes

MAKES 6 PINTS

8 cups thinly sliced green tomatoes

3 large onions, thinly sliced

¼ cup salt

6 pint-size canning jars, lids and screw-on bands

2 broken (3") cinnamon sticks

1 tablespoon black peppercorns

1 tablespoon whole cloves

1 tablespoon whole allspice

1 tablespoon celery seeds

1 tablespoon mustard seeds

3 cups apple cider vinegar

1 pound light brown sugar

2 red bell peppers, thinly sliced

1 In a large glass or plastic bowl, combine tomatoes and onions. Sprinkle with salt. Cover, and refrigerate overnight.

2 The following day, remove from the refrigerator. Add enough cold water to cover tomatoes and onions. Let vegetables stand in water for 1 hour.

3 Sterilize canning jars, lids and screw-on bands in boiling water for at least 5 minutes. Drain well.

4 Make a cheesecloth bundle to enclose the cinnamon, peppercorns, cloves, allspice, celery seeds and mustard seeds. Secure shut with kitchen twine.

5 In a Dutch oven, combine vinegar and brown sugar. Bring to a boil, stirring to dissolve the sugar. Add cheesecloth bundle, reduce heat to simmer, and cook 30 minutes.

6 Add tomatoes and onions. Bring to a low boil, and simmer over low heat 30 minutes. Remove and discard cheesecloth bundle.

7 Evenly distribute tomatoes and onions among canning jars. Evenly divide strips of red bell peppers among jars, standing strips on end around inside perimeter of jar. Divide spiced vinegar syrup among jars, coming to within ½" of tops of jars.

8 Wipe rims clean, and add jar lids, securing with the screw-on bands. Carefully lower the filled canning jars into a large canning pot. Cover jars by at least 1" of boiling water. Boil gently 15 minutes.

> **NOTE:** One of my guilty pleasures after a long day at the restaurant is a sandwich made using these pickled green tomatoes and thinly sliced smoked cheddar cheese on toasted wheat bread lavished with mayonnaise. Oh, and a heavy grinding of fresh black pepper, too. You gotta trust the chef with this one! It really is a divine (although quirky) combination.

Dana Sue's Pickled Okra

MAKES 3 PINTS

3 (1-pint) wide-mouth canning jars, lids and screw-on bands

9 peeled garlic cloves, divided

3 teaspoons crushed red pepper flakes, divided

3 bay leaves, divided

3 teaspoons dill weed, divided

3 tablespoons sugar, divided

3 teaspoons salt, divided

2 pounds okra

1½ cups water

1½ cups apple cider vinegar

1 Sterilize the canning jars, lids and screw-on bands in boiling water for at least 5 minutes. Remove jars, lids and bands from water to drain.

2 In the bottom of each jar, layer the ingredients as follows:
① 3 garlic cloves
② 1 teaspoon crushed red pepper flakes
③ 1 bay leaf
④ 1 teaspoon dill weed
⑤ 1 tablespoon sugar
⑥ 1 teaspoon salt

3 Divide okra among the jars, standing okra upright.

4 Combine water and vinegar. Bring to a full boil. Pour over the okra.

5 Wipe rims of jars clean. Place lids on jars, and secure with screw-on bands. Place in a pot of boiling water, making sure water covers the jars by at least 1". Boil for 15 minutes.

6 Carefully remove jars from boiling water, and let stand at room temperature 30 minutes. Turn jars upside down, and cool for another 30 minutes. Turn jars upright, and cool completely.

7 Check jars for a tight vacuum seal. If any of the jars did not seal, refrigerate for use within 2 weeks. Store sealed jars at room temperature for up to 1 year before using.

> **NOTE:** Honey, down South we pickle just about anything! This same recipe is great using fresh whole green beans instead of okra, but we Southerners are mighty fond of our okra. Use this pickled okra as a great little nibble—anywhere you would normally use dill pickles. A piece of this pickled okra makes a Bloody Mary extra special.

Pickled Dilly Green Beans

MAKES 5 PINTS

5 pint-size canning jars, lids and metal bands

3 (14-ounce) bags frozen whole green beans, thawed, rinsed and drained well or 3 pounds fresh green beans, stem ends trimmed and discarded

5 whole garlic cloves

5 sprigs fresh dill weed or 5 teaspoons dried

5 small dried hot red peppers or 2½ teaspoons crushed red pepper flakes

2½ cups distilled white vinegar

1 cup sugar

¼ cup salt

1 Wash, rinse, and sterilize 5 jars, lids and metal bands.

2 Pack beans vertically in jars. To each jar, add 1 garlic clove, 1 dill sprig (or 1 teaspoon dried) and 1 hot pepper (or ½ teaspoon pepper flakes).

3 Bring vinegar, sugar and salt to a boil over high heat, stirring to dissolve salt and sugar. Pour hot liquid over the beans.

4 Wipe jar rims clean. Top with lids, and secure tightly with bands. Cool to room temperature. Refrigerate at least 1 week and up to 1 month.

NOTE: These are the ultimate garnish for a Bloody Mary!

Fresh Apple Cake

SERVES 16

1½ cups canola oil

1 pound light brown sugar

3 eggs, beaten

1 teaspoon pure almond extract

1 teaspoon pure vanilla extract

3 cups all-purpose flour

1 teaspoon salt

1 teaspoon baking soda

1 tablespoon apple pie spice

6 cups diced Gala apples, peeled or unpeeled (you decide!)

1 cup chopped walnuts

1 Preheat oven to 325°F.

2 Grease and flour a 12-cup Bundt pan.

3 In a large mixing bowl, beat oil and sugar 2 minutes. Add eggs and extracts.

4 In a medium mixing bowl, whisk together flour, salt, baking soda and apple pie spice. Add flour mixture to the batter, and blend well. Stir in apples and walnuts by hand using a wooden spoon.

5 Spoon batter into prepared pan. Bake 90 minutes, until tester inserted in center comes out clean.

6 Cool in pan on rack 10 minutes. Remove from pan, and cool thoroughly. Store airtight at room temperature up to 3 days.

> **NOTE:** This cake is quite versatile and so tasty. Serve it as a dessert topped with vanilla bean ice cream and drizzled with warm caramel sauce. It also makes a great after-school snack or breakfast pastry.

MAKE YOUR OWN APPLE PIE SPICE: Combine ½ cup ground cinnamon, 2 tablespoons ground nutmeg, 1 tablespoon ground allspice and 1 tablespoon ground cloves. Whisk together to blend. Store airtight at room temperature to use within 1 year.

Spring Pea Vichyssoise
with Vegetable Confetti

SERVES 6–8

SOUP

2 cups medium-diced sweet onion

2 tablespoons olive oil

1½ pounds peeled russet potatoes,
cut into 1" pieces

4 cups chicken broth

1 pound frozen baby peas

1 cup heavy whipping cream, divided

Salt and white pepper to taste

CONFETTI

Tiny-diced multicolored bell peppers

1. In a heavy large saucepan over medium heat, sauté onions in oil.

2. Add potatoes and chicken broth. Bring to a boil. Reduce heat, cover, and simmer until potatoes are very tender, stirring occasionally, about 15 minutes.

3. Add peas, cover, and continue cooking until just tender, about 5 minutes.

4. Working in batches, puree soup in blender. Transfer to a bowl. Cool slightly. Chill uncovered until cold, then cover, and chill. (Can be made 1 day ahead. Keep chilled.)

5. Before serving, whisk in ¾ cup whipping cream. Season with salt and white pepper. Thin soup with more broth, if desired. Ladle soup into bowls. Drizzle remaining ¼ cup whipping cream on top of soup, then garnish with bell peppers.

> **NOTE:** Although this soup is great served warm, I much prefer to serve it cold in chilled soup bowls. It's so pretty and so good. For the diet conscious, you can substitute fat-free half-and-half for the whipping cream.

Vidalia Onion Canapés

MAKES ABOUT 40

2 cups grated Vidalia onion, squeezed dry

1 cup freshly grated Parmesan cheese

1 cup mayonnaise

½ teaspoon cayenne pepper

1 very thinly sliced 16-ounce loaf cocktail party pumpernickel or rye bread

Paprika

1 Blend first 4 ingredients. Cover, and refrigerate several hours or up to 1 week before using.

2 Preheat oven to 350°F.

3 Spread heaping tablespoon of mixture evenly on each bread slice. Place in single layer on baking sheet. Sprinkle tops lightly with paprika.

4 Bake 15–20 minutes or until topping is puffed and golden. Serve hot or warm.

Lavender Blue Dilly Dilly Green Bean Salad

SERVES 8–10

SALAD

2 pounds fresh baby green beans, stem ends removed

½ cup thinly sliced radishes

½ cup chopped walnuts

½ cup blue cheese crumbles

1 cup chopped green onions

DRESSING

¼ cup minced fresh dill weed

3 tablespoons sugar

3 tablespoons lemon juice

2 tablespoons Dijon mustard

2 tablespoons minced fresh parsley

2 tablespoons apple cider vinegar

1 teaspoon food-safe dried lavender

¾ cup extra-virgin olive oil

Salt and pepper to taste

Salad

Steam green beans until crisp tender. Immerse beans in a bowl filled with ice water to stop cooking, and drain well. Combine with remaining salad ingredients in a large serving bowl.

Dressing

Process first 7 ingredients in blender or food processor. With machine running, pour olive oil in a thin, steady stream through the top, and blend 30 seconds. Season to taste with salt and pepper. Pour dressing over green bean salad, and toss to coat. Refrigerate at least 4 hours or up to 3 days before serving.

Apple Salad
with Sherry & Honey Vinaigrette

MAKES 2 CUPS

Kosher salt

Mixed greens (optional)

SALAD

3 Gala apples

1 cup thinly sliced celery

1 cup golden raisins
or dried, sweetened cranberries

1 cup pecan pieces, toasted

1 (4-ounce) package
blue cheese crumbles

VINAIGRETTE

½ cup sherry vinegar or ¼ cup
apple cider vinegar + ¼ cup sherry

¼ cup honey

1 tablespoon coarse-grain Dijon
mustard

1 garlic clove, minced

1 cup vegetable oil

½ cup extra-virgin olive oil

Freshly ground black pepper to taste

Salad

1. Fill a bowl halfway with water. Add enough salt to taste like seawater, stirring to dissolve.
2. Core and cut apples into bite-size pieces. Immediately soak in salted water for a couple of minutes to keep apples from turning brown.
3. Drain well, but do not rinse.
4. Toss with remaining salad ingredients, and coat well with sherry & honey vinaigrette. Serve as is or over mixed greens.

Vinaigrette

Combine first 4 ingredients in blender or food processor. With machine running, add oils in a thin, steady stream. Season with salt and pepper.

Oven-Roasted Sweet Potato Tailgate Salad

SERVES 6

4½ cups peeled, cubed sweet potatoes

6 tablespoons extra-virgin olive oil, divided

Sea salt

¼ cup honey

¼ cup white wine vinegar

1 tablespoon minced fresh rosemary

2 garlic cloves, minced

Salt and pepper to taste

1. Preheat oven to 450°F.

2. Line a 15" × 10" jelly-roll pan with nonstick foil. Toss together potato cubes and 2 tablespoons olive oil in pan. Sprinkle with sea salt. Scatter on pan.

3. Roast 35 minutes or until fork tender. Cool to room temperature.

4. Whisk together remaining ingredients. Add cooled, roasted potatoes, and toss well. Serve slightly chilled or at room temperature. Cover, and refrigerate up to 4 days.

> **NOTE:** This recipe is always such a hit. It's especially great for fall picnics and tailgates—and no mayonnaise to worry about!

Lowcountry Seafood Gumbo

SERVES 8–10

¾ cup vegetable oil

¾ cup all-purpose flour

2 cups diced onions, divided

1 cup diced bell pepper, divided

1 cup thinly sliced celery, divided

¼ cup minced parsley, divided

4–6 garlic cloves, minced

1 tablespoon Cajun and Creole seasoning

4 cups fish or chicken stock

1 (20-ounce) package frozen creamed white corn, thawed

1 (14½-ounce) can diced tomatoes

2 bay leaves

1 pound fresh or frozen peeled, deveined shrimp

1 pound fresh or frozen white fish filets

8 ounces fresh crabmeat, picked through

2 tablespoons gumbo filé powder

Salt and freshly ground black pepper to taste

Steamed rice (optional)

Roux

1 In a large Dutch oven over medium-high heat, combine oil and flour. Whisk until smooth. Stir constantly. (**Caution:** Spattering roux can cause painful burns!)

2 When the roux has reached the color of milk chocolate, add half the onions, bell pepper, celery and parsley. Cook and stir 2–3 minutes.

3 Stir in garlic and Cajun and Creole seasoning. Add stock, corn, tomatoes and bay leaves. Bring to a boil. Reduce heat, and simmer 10–15 minutes.

4 Stir in seafood and remaining onions, bell pepper, celery and parsley. Cook just until seafood is cooked through. Season with filé powder, salt and pepper. Serve with or without steamed rice.

Southern Smothered Corn Chowder

SERVES 8

2 medium red-skinned potatoes, diced into ½" cubes

3 cups water

6 slices bacon, cut into thin strips

1 cup finely diced onion

2 (20-ounce) packages frozen creamed white corn, thawed

4 cups half-and-half

1 cup chicken stock

⅛ teaspoon ground nutmeg

Salt and pepper to taste

1 Bring potato cubes and 3 cups water to a boil in a large Dutch oven, reduce heat, and cook until potato cubes are cooked through. Remove from heat and set aside. (Do not drain.)

2 Cook bacon in a small Dutch oven or large saucepan until crisp. Using a slotted utensil, remove bacon from pan, and reserve drippings in pan.

3 Sauté onions in drippings until tender. Stir in remaining ingredients. Bring to a boil over medium heat, stirring often.

4 Add potato cubes and their cooking water to the soup. Return to a boil. Reduce heat to low, and simmer 5–10 minutes.

5 Ladle into bowls, garnishing each with the cooked bacon.

Cornmeal-Crusted Fried Okra

SERVES 6

¾ cup cornmeal

¾ cup all-purpose flour

1 tablespoon sugar

2 teaspoons seasoned salt

1 teaspoon freshly ground
black pepper

1 pound fresh okra

½ cup buttermilk

1 egg, beaten

¾ cup canola or vegetable oil

1 Combine cornmeal, flour, sugar, salt and pepper in a mixing bowl. Whisk until blended.

2 Trim ends from okra, and discard. Slice okra into ½" pieces. Place sliced okra in cornmeal mixture, and toss to coat. Remove okra from mixture, shaking off excess.

3 Whisk together buttermilk and egg until smooth. Place okra in egg mixture, and toss to coat. Transfer okra back to cornmeal mixture, and toss to coat and cling. Transfer coated okra to a surface lined with paper towels.

4 Heat oil in a heavy skillet over medium-high heat. Test oil to make sure it is hot enough to fry properly. Place a single piece of coated okra in hot oil. It should sizzle and bob around. Working in single-layer batches, carefully place coated okra in hot oil. When golden brown on underside, flip okra over, and cook on other side. When golden brown on both sides, remove from skillet with a slotted utensil, and place on surface lined with paper towels to drain. Sprinkle lightly with seasoned salt or sea salt. Enjoy immediately.

> **NOTE:** The coating method in this recipe is known as dry-wet-dry. It is the secret to the cornmeal coating staying on the okra during the frying process. Use this same method for any cornmeal-crusted garden veggie—fried green tomatoes, zucchini, yellow squash, Vidalia onion rings, etc.

Fall Harvest Bisque

SERVES 10

2 medium butternut squash, peeled, seeded, diced

6 cups chicken stock

2 cups apple juice or cider

1 (3") cinnamon stick

2 teaspoons minced fresh rosemary

2 cups apple sauce

2 cups whipping cream or half-and-half

¼ cup maple syrup

1 teaspoon vanilla extract

½ teaspoon grated nutmeg

Salt and white pepper to taste

In a Dutch oven, combine first 5 ingredients. Bring to a boil over medium-high heat. Reduce heat and simmer until squash is tender. Remove cinnamon stick. Using blender or food processor, puree in batches. Return mixture to Dutch oven. Add remaining ingredients, and cook until heated through, stirring occasionally. Do not boil.

Fresh Peach Macaroon Tarts

SERVES 6

CRUST

3 large egg whites

1 cup sugar

30 coarsely crushed Ritz crackers

1 cup chopped pecans

1 teaspoon almond extract

FILLING

1 cup cold heavy whipping cream

1 (8-ounce) package cream cheese, softened

1 cup confectioners' sugar

PEACHES

4 large or 6 medium peaches, thinly sliced

½ cup melted peach preserves or jam

1 teaspoon almond extract

TOPPING

1 cup cold heavy whipping cream

¼ cup confectioners' sugar

½ teaspoon almond extract

GARNISH

Grated nutmeg

Cinnamon

Crust

1 Preheat oven to 350°F.

2 Beat egg whites until frothy. Gradually add sugar, beating all the while. Beat until stiff peaks form.

3 Stir in remaining ingredients.

4 Draw 6 (5") circles on a piece of baking parchment. Turn parchment over, and place on baking sheet. Distribute meringue mixture evenly among the 6 circles, spreading to fill the circles. Bake 20 minutes.

5 Remove from oven, and let cool completely on parchment. Once cooled, store airtight until serving time. Can be prepared earlier in the day.

Filling

Combine ingredients in a medium mixing bowl. Beat until smooth. Cover, and refrigerate at least 1 hour.

Peaches

Combine ingredients in a medium mixing bowl. Stir gently to coat peaches. Cover, and refrigerate at least 1 hour.

Topping

Combine ingredients in a small mixing bowl. Beat until stiff peaks form. Cover, and refrigerate.

Assembly

Place macaroons on 6 dessert plates. Evenly distribute filling over crusts, and spread to the edges. Spoon peaches over the filling. Top each tart with a dollop of topping.

Garnish

Dust with freshly grated nutmeg or a sprinkling of cinnamon.

Sullivan's Smothered Corn

with Frizzled Bacon

SERVES 10–12

6 thick slices pepper-coated bacon, cut into thin strips

2 cups medium-diced sweet onion

1 cup medium-diced celery

1 red bell pepper, seeded, chopped

1 tablespoon minced garlic

¼ cup flour

1 tablespoon ham base

½ cup water

2 (20-ounce) packages frozen creamed white corn, thawed

½ teaspoon freshly ground black pepper

1 In a large deep skillet or Dutch oven over medium-high heat, cook bacon until crisp. Using a slotted cooking utensil, carefully transfer cooked bacon to a plate lined with paper towels, and reserve the drippings in the pan. Set aside the bacon.

2 In the drippings, sauté onion, celery, bell pepper and garlic until wilted and slightly cooked.

3 Sprinkle on flour, and stir into sautéed vegetables. Cook and stir constantly 1 minute or so.

4 Dissolve ham base in ½ cup water. Stir into vegetable mixture until smooth.

5 Add corn and black pepper. Reduce heat to medium, and continue to cook 10–15 minutes, stirring occasionally. Add additional water if necessary to prevent sticking to pan. Just before serving, stir cooked bacon into the corn. Serve hot.

Sunday Brunch
at Sullivan's

Folks here in Serenity have always had their big meal of the day just after church on Sunday. Some had it at home. Others packed the local restaurants.

For the longest time after I opened the doors at Sullivan's, I went along with tradition, serving the usual sort of Sunday meals with meat and potatoes and piping hot yeast rolls. Or maybe that old staple, fried chicken just like Grandma used to make. Then it occurred to me that Sullivan's has a reputation for shaking things up, doing the unexpected, not serving the exact same Sunday dinners folks could get if they went straight on home, put on their aprons and fixed a meal. The idea of putting a Sunday brunch on the menu, while not exactly revolutionary, was a real eye-opener here in town.

But think about it for a minute. How often do most people really take the time to cook a fancy breakfast these days? In our house, before I had my own restaurant, Ronnie was the one who whipped up a batch of pancakes on Sunday. Weekdays, during those years I was a single mom with Ronnie gone, I barely had time to pour a bowl of cereal or scramble an egg before sending Annie off to school.

But the truth is, most folks I know love a traditional breakfast as long as somebody else is cooking it. In Sullivan's we've taken that reality and kicked it up another notch or two with a mix of breakfast favorites and a few lunch specialties that aren't on our regular menu.

Now you can do the exact same thing when you have company visiting and want to sit right there at the kitchen table and linger over a glass of sweet tea and a few tasty dishes you'd never take the time to fix on an ordinary morning. After all, isn't the best part of having out-of-town guests taking the time to sit and visit over a leisurely meal—something we rarely get to do in our harried lives? I'm even sharing my own favorite sweet tea recipe to add an authentic touch to your Southern brunch.

When folks come into Sullivan's on Sunday, we give them a pastry basket of my almond-filled croissants and cranberry-orange scones with orange glaze and cranberry-orange butter. We offer miniature versions. After all, we certainly wouldn't want them to fill up on those, not with strawberry-topped stuffed French toast on the menu or a country ham and grits quiche. The recipes here are for the full-sized versions, of course. You'll probably want to pick and choose among the recipes. Try them all at once, and you'll be as stuffed as that delicious French toast.

Of course, some folks here at Sullivan's opt for the pineapple chicken salad, especially if they had breakfast at home before going to church. And you can't very well call it brunch if you're not offering a combination of breakfast and lunch choices, so we always include a variety of specials that cater to folks who can't bear to break with their old Sunday traditions.

Whatever you put on your own Sunday brunch menu, just be sure to include a warm helping of Southern hospitality. It'll keep your visitors coming back time and again.

Dana Sue's Almond-Filled Croissants

MAKES 8

8 medium croissants

1 cup sliced almonds, divided

½ cup sugar, divided

¼ cup (2 ounces) almond paste

6 tablespoons butter, softened

3 large egg yolks

1 teaspoon pure almond extract

Confectioners' sugar

1 Preheat oven to 350°F.

2 Split croissants in half horizontally. Using a food processor, combine ½ cup almonds and ¼ cup sugar. Process until finely ground. Add almond paste, and process until finely chopped.

3 Using an electric mixer, cream together butter and remaining ¼ cup sugar. Add almond mixture, and beat at medium speed 1 minute. Beat in egg yolks and almond extract.

4 Fill each croissant with 2 tablespoons almond filling, heaping in the center and spreading to the edges. Sandwich croissant together with filling in center. Spread 1 tablespoon filling over top of each croissant. Press tops of each croissant into remaining ½ cup almonds. Place on parchment or foil-lined baking sheet a couple of inches apart.

5 Bake 20 minutes or until tops are deep golden brown and almonds on top are toasted. Serve warm or at room temperature, garnished with a slight dusting of confectioners' sugar.

Classic Cream Scones

MAKES 24 PETITE SCONES

2 cups all-purpose flour

½ cup granulated sugar

1 tablespoon baking powder

1 teaspoon salt

½ cup cold butter, cut into cubes

1 cup heavy whipping cream

1 teaspoon pure vanilla extract

½ teaspoon pure almond extract

Egg wash (1 beaten egg
+ 2 tablespoons water)

Coarse sugar

1 Preheat oven to 425°F.

2 In a food processor fitted with the chopping blade, combine first 4 ingredients.

3 Add butter and operate food processor in 1-second pulses until butter is the size of small peas. (Alternatively, cut butter into dry ingredients using a handheld pastry blender.)

4 Transfer dry ingredients to a mixing bowl. Make a well in the center of dry ingredients.

5 In a small mixing bowl, combine whipping cream and extracts. Pour into well. Stir just until dough clings together.

6 Transfer dough to a floured work surface. Roll dough to ½" thickness.

7 Using a 2" round cutter, cut out dough. Place on a parchment-lined baking sheet 1" apart. Brush tops with egg wash. Sprinkle tops with coarse sugar.

8 Bake 10–12 minutes until tops are golden.

9 Remove from oven, and transfer to cooling rack. Serve warm.

Frosted Café Royale

SERVES 20 Recipe halves easily for smaller gatherings.

½ gallon (8 cups) double-strength freshly brewed coffee

2 cups sugar

2 cups brandy

1 quart half-and-half

2 cups milk

½ gallon vanilla ice cream

In a gallon-size container, combine coffee and sugar. Stir to dissolve. Add brandy. Bring to room temperature, then cover, and refrigerate until thoroughly chilled. Add half-and-half and milk. Serve over ice cream cut into 1" cubes.

> **NOTE:** To make a frosted mocha royale, simply substitute 2 cups chocolate milk for the milk, and use chocolate ice cream instead of vanilla.

Lemon & Poppy Seed Scones

MAKES 24 PETITE SCONES

SCONES

2½ cups self-rising flour

½ cup granulated sugar

2 teaspoons baking powder

½ cup cold, cubed unsalted butter

Grated zest of 2 lemons

2 tablespoons poppy seeds

1 cup heavy whipping cream

1 teaspoon vanilla extract

Yellow food coloring (optional)

GLAZE

2 cups sifted confectioners' sugar

Lemon juice

Yellow food coloring (optional)

Scones

1 Preheat oven to 425°F.

2 In food processor fitted with the chopping blade, combine first 3 ingredients.

3 Add butter and lemon zest. Operate food processor in 1-second pulses until the butter is the size of small peas. (Alternatively, cut butter into dry ingredients using a handheld pastry blender.)

4 Transfer dry ingredients to a mixing bowl. Stir in poppy seeds. Make a well in the center of dry ingredients.

5 In a small bowl, blend together whipping cream, vanilla extract and food coloring. Pour into the well of dry ingredients. Stir until the dough clings together—it will be very stiff!

6 Transfer dough to a floured work surface, and roll to ¾" thickness.

7 Using a 2" round cutter, cut out dough. Place on a parchment-lined baking sheet at least 1" apart.

8 Bake 10–12 minutes or until tops are golden brown. While scones are baking, prepare glaze.

9 Remove from oven, and immediately transfer scones to a cooling rack.

Glaze

Sift confectioners' sugar into a small bowl. Adding a little bit of lemon juice at a time, stir until a thick glaze is formed. Tint with a few drops of food coloring. While scones are still warm, spread tops with glaze. Let glaze set several minutes. Serve warm.

Cranberry-Orange Scones

with Orange Glaze

MAKES 12 LARGE SCONES

SCONES

2½ cups self-rising flour

½ cup granulated sugar

Grated zest of 2 oranges

½ teaspoon ground cinnamon

½ teaspoon ground ginger

⅛ teaspoon ground nutmeg

⅛ teaspoon ground cloves

½ cup cubed cold butter

¾ cup pecan pieces

¾ cup dried, sweetened cranberries (such as Craisins)

1 cup heavy whipping cream

GLAZE

2 cups sifted confectioners' sugar

Grated zest of 1 orange

2–3 tablespoons orange juice

Scones

1 Combine first 7 ingredients.

2 Preheat oven to 425°F.

3 Using a handheld pastry blender or a food processor, cut in butter until the butter is the size of small peas.

4 Stir in pecan pieces and cranberries. Make a well in center of dough.

5 Pour whipping cream into the center of the well. Blend until dough comes together, but do not overmix.

6 On a lightly floured surface, divide dough in half, and form each half into a 6" circle. Cut each circle into 6 pie-shaped wedges. Place 2" apart on a greased or parchment-lined baking sheet.

7 Bake 15–18 minutes until tops are golden brown and centers of scones test done. Prepare glaze while scones are baking.

8 Remove from oven, and transfer scones to a cooling rack.

Glaze

Place confectioners' sugar and orange zest in a small mixing bowl. Add enough orange juice to make a very thick glaze. After scones have cooled for 5 minutes, spread glaze on top of scones. Let glaze harden. Serve warm. Store in an airtight container.

Gingerbread Scones

MAKES 12

2¼ cups all-purpose flour

¼ packed cup light brown sugar

2 tablespoons finely minced crystallized ginger

1 teaspoon baking powder

1 teaspoon ground ginger

1 teaspoon ground cinnamon

½ teaspoon baking soda

¼ teaspoon ground nutmeg

⅛ teaspoon ground cloves

½ cup cubed, cold butter

¾ cup heavy whipping cream

⅓ cup molasses

1 Preheat oven to 425°F.

2 Combine all ingredients except butter, cream and molasses, and whisk to blend.

3 Using a handheld pastry blender, cut butter into dry ingredients until the butter is the size of peas.

4 Whisk together the whipping cream and molasses. Add to the dry ingredients. Stir just until dough clings together.

5 Turn dough out onto a lightly floured work surface, and knead several times.

6 Divide dough into 2 equal pieces. Shape each piece into a flat 6" round. Cut each round into 6 pie-shaped wedges. Place on a baking sheet, spacing a couple of inches apart.

7 Bake in center of oven for about 15 minutes.

Cranberry-Orange Butter

MAKES 2 CUPS

1 cup butter, room temperature

½ cup orange marmalade

½ cup finely chopped dried, sweetened cranberries (such as Craisins)

Combine butter and orange marmalade in a small bowl. Using an electric mixer, blend well. Add cranberries, and blend until thoroughly incorporated.

> **NOTE:** Serve at room temperature with biscuits, toast and especially scones! It also makes a deliciously simple spread for gingersnaps.

Macaroon Muffins

with Dates & Pecans

MAKES 12

3 egg whites at room temperature

⅔ cup sugar

1 cup coarsely crushed vanilla wafers

1 cup chopped pecans

½ cup pitted, chopped dates

1 teaspoon almond extract

½ teaspoon baking powder

1 Preheat oven to 350°F.

2 Beat egg whites until foamy. Continue beating, adding the sugar gradually, until stiff peaks form and most of the sugar has dissolved.

3 Fold in remaining ingredients until well blended.

4 Divide mixture evenly among 12 paper-lined muffin cups.

5 Bake 18–20 minutes or until tops are golden brown and cake tester inserted in center comes out clean.

6 Allow to cool in pan 10 minutes, then remove from pan, and continue cooling on rack. Store airtight.

> **NOTE:** To serve these muffins as a wonderful light dessert, omit the dates, and bake as directed. When ready to serve, remove muffins from paper, and split in half. Spoon on fresh fruit (sweetened, if desired) and lots of freshly whipped cream.

Lowcountry Crab Hash

SERVES 4–6

1½ pounds washed red-skinned potatoes, cut into ½" cubes

OLD BAY Seasoning

3 thick slices smoked pepper-coated bacon, cut into thin strips

1 cup medium-diced onion

1 bell pepper, medium-diced

8 ounces fresh crabmeat, picked over

½ cup minced fresh parsley

Freshly ground black pepper to taste

1 Cook potatoes in boiling water seasoned with OLD BAY until just fork tender; do not overcook. Shock in cold water, or pour into a colander and run cold water over potatoes several minutes to stop their cooking. Drain well. (This can be done 1 day ahead and then refrigerated.)

2 In a large skillet, cook bacon until crisp. Remove from skillet, reserving drippings in pan.

3 In drippings, cook onions until translucent. Add bell pepper and potatoes, and heat through, stirring to coat.

4 Just before serving, stir in crabmeat, parsley and cooked bacon. Season to taste with additional OLD BAY Seasoning and freshly ground black pepper.

> **NOTE:** This hash is a favorite Lowcountry breakfast or brunch dish. It is extra delicious (and indulgent!) to top each serving with a poached egg, then spoon hollandaise sauce on top.

Microwave Lemon Curd

MAKES 4 CUPS

2 cups sugar

12 large egg yolks

1 cup freshly squeezed lemon juice

¼ cup freshly grated lemon zest

1 cup butter, room temperature

Whisk together sugar, egg yolks, lemon juice and lemon zest. Cook in microwave on high (100% power) until mixture boils, stirring well after each minute of cooking. Bring to room temperature. Beat in butter, a couple of tablespoons at a time. Beat until smooth. Cover, and refrigerate up to 1 month.

Stuffed French Toast

with Glazed Strawberries

SERVES 6–8

FILLING

1 (8-ounce) package cream cheese, softened

1 cup whole-milk ricotta cheese

¼ cup sugar

FRENCH TOAST

1 large loaf French bread, thinly sliced

1 cup half-and-half

4 eggs, beaten

¼ teaspoon salt

2 teaspoons vanilla

¼ teaspoon ground cinnamon

⅛ teaspoon ground nutmeg

½ cup clarified butter

STRAWBERRIES

1 pound fresh strawberries

¾ cup strawberry jam

¼ cup orange marmalade

Filling

Blend all ingredients until smooth.

French Toast

1 Spread filling on half the number of bread slices. Top with remaining slices, and press together. Arrange a few in a single layer in a shallow pan.

2 Whisk together remaining ingredients except butter. Pour over stuffed bread. Soak briefly on both sides.

3 Fry slices in clarified butter until golden brown, turning once. Transfer to a warm serving platter. Cover.

4 Repeat with remaining stuffed bread slices.

Strawberries

1 Trim away caps from strawberries and discard. Thinly slice the strawberries.

2 Blend together strawberry jam and orange marmalade. Pour over the sliced strawberries. Stir gently to coat the strawberry slices.

3 Spoon the strawberry and jam topping over each serving of prepared French toast.

Spicy Shrimp & Sausage

with Country Ham Cream-Style Gravy over Creamy Yellow Grits

SERVES 8

CREAMY GRITS

1 quart half-and-half

1 quart whole milk

2 cups coarsely ground yellow grits

½ cup butter

2 tablespoons sugar

1 tablespoon salt

Pepper to taste

COUNTRY HAM GRAVY

¼ cup butter

½ cup all-purpose flour

1 quart half-and-half

2 tablespoons ham base or bouillon

3 ounces country ham, chopped

SHRIMP & SAUSAGE

1½ pounds andouille or smoked sausage

1½ pounds peeled, deveined shrimp

2 tablespoons butter

2 tablespoons Cajun and Creole seasoning

¼ cup whipping cream

GARNISH (OPTIONAL)

¼ cup chopped fresh parsley

Grits

1 Combine all ingredients in a large saucepan. Bring to a boil over medium-high heat, stirring frequently and breaking up any lumps with a whisk.

2 Reduce heat, cover, and simmer at least 20 minutes, stirring often. Adjust seasoning if necessary. Prepare the gravy while the grits are cooking.

Gravy

1 Melt butter in heavy saucepan over medium heat. Add flour, stirring constantly, 2–4 minutes or until lightly browned.

2 Gradually add half-and-half and ham base, whisking constantly. Cook until mixture has thickened. Stir in chopped country ham.

3 Cover, and simmer 10–15 minutes, stirring occasionally. While the grits and the gravy are simmering, prepare the shrimp & sausage.

Shrimp & Sausage

1 Cut sausage into ½"-thick rounds. In a large skillet, cook thoroughly over medium-high heat. Drain, and set aside.

2 In a large skillet, cook shrimp in butter and Cajun and Creole seasoning over medium-high heat 3–5 minutes, just until shrimp blush and curl.

3 Add sausage and 2½ cups prepared gravy. Cook over medium heat 1–2 minutes.

4 Stir in whipping cream, and cook until heated through. If mixture is too thick, add a bit of milk to thin down.

To Serve

Spoon about 1 cup grits into a large shallow bowl or onto a plate, and spoon shrimp and sausage mixture over grits. Sprinkle with parsley. Serve with additional gravy on the side.

Chicken Salad

with Dijon-Dill Dressing & Toasted Almonds

SERVES 4

SALAD

¾ cup slivered almonds

3 cups diced, cooked chicken breast

3 stalks celery, thinly sliced

1 bunch green onions (white and light green parts only), thinly sliced

8 leaves Boston or butter lettuce

DRESSING

1 cup mayonnaise

1 tablespoon Dijon mustard

1 tablespoon minced fresh dill weed or 1 teaspoon dried

1 teaspoon salt

½ teaspoon freshly ground black pepper

Salad

Preheat oven to 350°F. Scatter almonds on a baking sheet. Bake about 10 minutes, just until nuts are lightly browned and begin to smell toasted. Cool to room temperature, and set aside. In a medium mixing bowl, combine chicken, celery and green onions.

Dressing

In a small mixing bowl, whisk all dressing ingredients together. Transfer dressing to chicken salad. Stir to blend well. Cover, and refrigerate at least 2 hours or up to 3 days before serving.

To Serve

Just before serving, stir toasted almonds into chicken salad. Place 2 lettuce leaves on each of 4 salad or luncheon plates. Place a large scoop of chicken salad on top.

Pineapple Chicken Salad

MAKES 8

SALAD

2 medium fresh pineapples (whole with tops)

2 cups cubed, cooked chicken breast

⅔ cup thinly sliced celery

⅔ cup seedless green grapes, cut in half lengthwise

½ cup sweetened flaked coconut

½ cup coarsely chopped, roasted, salted macadamia nuts

DRESSING

1 (8-ounce) package cream cheese, softened

¾ cup mayonnaise

3 tablespoons orange marmalade

Salad

1 Using a very sharp knife, slice pineapple in half lengthwise. Slice each half into two quarters lengthwise. Repeat with other pineapple.

2 Using a sharp knife, remove most of the flesh of each pineapple quarter, leaving a substantial shell (boat shaped) that will hold the prepared chicken salad. Remove core from each piece of pineapple.

3 Cut remaining pineapple flesh into bite-size cubes. Turn pineapple boats upside down on paper towels to drain.

4 Combine pineapple chunks with all remaining salad ingredients except nuts.

Dressing

Combine all dressing ingredients, and blend together using a whisk or an electric mixer. Pour over salad ingredients. Stir gently but thoroughly to blend well.

To Serve

Scoop an equal amount of prepared chicken salad into each of 8 pineapple boats. Sprinkle macadamia nuts over top. Serve immediately.

Barbecue Salad

with Tangy Coleslaw

SERVES 4-6

COLESLAW

1 (10-ounce) package coleslaw mix

⅓ cup mayonnaise

¼ cup prepared ranch dressing

¼ cup wine vinegar

¼ cup sugar

1½ teaspoons garlic salt

½ teaspoon freshly ground black pepper

BARBECUE SALAD

2 hearts of romaine, thinly sliced

2 cups fully cooked, shredded pork barbecue in sauce, warmed slightly

1 Prepare coleslaw 1 day ahead of serving. Place coleslaw mix in a medium mixing bowl.

2 Combine remaining slaw ingredients in a small bowl. Whisk together.

3 Pour over slaw mix. Stir to coat well. Cover, and refrigerate at least 4 hours.

4 Just prior to serving, arrange lettuce on a serving platter or on 4 individual plates. Spoon warmed barbecue over lettuce. Top with coleslaw.

> **NOTE:** I usually purchase the pork barbecue at a favorite local barbecue restaurant, but I've also purchased it in grocery stores, in either the frozen food or canned meats section.

Sullivan's Crab Cakes

SERVES 6 as an entrée or 12 as an appetizer.

1 pound fresh lump crabmeat, picked through

1 stack Ritz crackers, coarsely crushed

½ cup mayonnaise

¼ cup chopped fresh parsley

2 eggs, beaten

1 tablespoon OLD BAY Seasoning

Finely grated zest of 1 lemon

Tabasco sauce to taste

¼ cup butter

1. In a mixing bowl, use your hands to carefully combine the crabmeat with the coarsely crushed crackers.

2. In another mixing bowl, whisk together all remaining ingredients except butter.

3. Blend gently with the crab and cracker mixture, being careful not to break up the crabmeat. Cover, and refrigerate at least 30 minutes or up to 1 day ahead.

4. Shape into crab cakes of desired size.

5. Fry in melted butter in a heavy-bottomed skillet over medium-high heat. Turn once when halfway through cooking. Cook until golden brown on both sides.

> **NOTE:** Chef Erik at Sullivan's serves these yummy crab cakes as a brunch specialty, topping each crab cake with a poached egg and a ladle of sherry hollandaise sauce over the crab cake (see next recipe). On the evening menu, the crab cakes are featured as a starter course and served with our Carolina rémoulade sauce (recipe follows).

Sherry Hollandaise Sauce

MAKES ABOUT 1½ CUPS

6 egg yolks

1 teaspoon salt

¼ teaspoon ground cayenne pepper

¼ cup sherry

1 cup butter, cubed, room temperature

Combine all but the butter in the top section of a double boiler. Stirring constantly, cook over simmering water until very hot. Whisk in butter one cube at a time until all butter has been incorporated and sauce is smooth. Transfer to a bowl or gravy boat. Cover with plastic wrap, then swaddle in a kitchen towel to keep warm until serving time (up to 15 minutes).

> **CHEF'S TIP:** To make a traditional hollandaise sauce, replace the sherry with freshly squeezed lemon juice. Finely grated lemon zest is a lovely addition as well.

Carolina Rémoulade Sauce

MAKES ABOUT 1 QUART

2 cups mayonnaise

½ cup prepared chili sauce

½ cup finely chopped green onions
(white and light green parts only)

⅓ cup Creole mustard

¼ cup extra-virgin olive oil

¼ cup finely chopped celery

¼ cup finely minced fresh parsley

Finely grated zest and juice of
1 medium lemon

1 tablespoon minced garlic

1 tablespoon minced capers

Salt and Tabasco sauce to taste

Prepare at least 1 hour ahead of serving time. (Best if made a day or so ahead to allow flavors to blend.) Combine all ingredients in a mixing bowl. Whisk to blend well. Cover, and refrigerate up to 2 weeks.

> **NOTE:** Okay, here's the scoop on rémoulade sauce. As with most sauces, it is French in origin but reached its height of popularity in New Orleans cuisine. Here in the South, we love this sauce on almost anything, but it is especially wonderful served with crab cakes, spicy boiled shrimp, fried green tomatoes and other fried veggies. It also makes a delicious spread for sandwiches and any fried seafood. Although the recipe makes almost 4 cups, you can prepare just a half batch if desired. Once you taste it, though, you'll wish you had prepared the full recipe.

Country Ham & Grits Quiche

with Red-Eye Gravy

SERVES 6–8

QUICHE

6 ounces country ham

½ cup water

½ teaspoon salt

⅓ cup uncooked quick-cooking grits

1 (12-ounce) can evaporated milk

1 cup (4 ounces) shredded sharp cheddar cheese

3 large eggs, beaten

1 teaspoon dry mustard powder

1 teaspoon Tabasco sauce

GRAVY

Pan drippings from country ham

2 cups very strong coffee

2 tablespoons butter

2 tablespoons cornstarch

¼ cup cold water

Salt and freshly ground black pepper to taste

Quiche

1 Preheat oven to 350°F.

2 Grease a deep-dish 9" pie plate.

3 In a skillet over medium-high heat, place country ham in enough water to cover. Cook 5 minutes, adding additional water as necessary.

4 Remove ham from skillet. Reserve water and pan drippings for gravy. Dice ham, and set aside.

5 In a large saucepan, bring ½ cup water and salt to a boil.

6 Stir in grits. Remove from heat, cover, and let stand 5 minutes (mixture will be very thick).

7 Stir in country ham and remaining ingredients. Pour into prepared pie plate.

8 Bake 30–35 minutes. Let stand 10 minutes before serving. Prepare gravy while quiche bakes.

Gravy

In the same skillet used to cook the ham, add the coffee and butter to the pan drippings. Cook over medium-high heat until reduced to 1 cup. Dissolve cornstarch in water. Quickly whisk into gravy. Stir constantly until thickened. Season to taste. Serve hot over wedges of quiche.
Makes 1¼ cups.

Crustless Broccoli & Three-Cheese Quiche

SERVES 6

2 cups milk

4 large eggs, beaten

¾ cup biscuit baking mix
(such as Bisquick)

4 tablespoons butter, softened

½ teaspoon freshly ground
black pepper

2 cups chopped, steamed crisp-
tender broccoli

1 cup canned French-fried onions

1 cup grated Parmesan cheese

1 cup grated Swiss cheese

1 cup grated cheddar cheese

1 Preheat oven to 375°F.

2 Grease a 10" quiche pan.

3 In a large mixing bowl using an electric mixer on low speed,
  blend together the first 5 ingredients.

4 Stir in broccoli, French-fried onions and the 3 grated cheeses.
  Transfer mixture to the prepared quiche pan.

5 Place in the center of the oven. Bake 45–50 minutes, until center
  is set and top is golden brown.

6 Remove from oven, and let stand 5 minutes before serving.

Caramelized Onion & Bacon Quiche

SERVES 6

CRUST

1½ cups finely crushed Ritz crackers

6 tablespoons unsalted butter, room temperature

FILLING

4 slices thick-sliced bacon, cut into thin strips

3 cups thinly sliced sweet onions

1 cup half-and-half

3 large eggs

1 teaspoon salt

½ teaspoon freshly ground black pepper

¼ teaspoon freshly grated nutmeg

6 ounces (1½ cups) grated Gruyère or Swiss cheese

GARNISH (OPTIONAL)

¼ cup minced fresh parsley

Crust

Preheat oven to 350°F. Combine ingredients until well blended. Press mixture in bottom and 1" up sides of a 9" pie plate. Bake 10 minutes. Prepare filling while crust bakes.

Filling

1 In a skillet over medium heat, cook bacon until crisp. Reserving drippings, use a slotted spoon to transfer bacon to a plate lined with paper towels.

2 In drippings, cook onions until tender, cooking away all liquid from onions. Arrange onions in cracker crust.

3 Beat half-and-half, eggs, salt, pepper and nutmeg in a medium bowl until blended. Pour egg mixture over onions in crust. Sprinkle cheese and cooked bacon over filling.

4 Bake until knife inserted into center comes out clean, about 40 minutes. Garnish with parsley, and serve.

Petite Dilly Biscuits

MAKES 24

3 cups Bisquick baking mix

1 cup sour cream

½ cup melted butter

2 tablespoons minced fresh dill weed
or 2 teaspoons dried

1 Preheat oven to 425°F.

2 Lightly grease or parchment-line a baking sheet.

3 Combine all ingredients in a medium mixing bowl. Stir to blend
using a wooden spoon.

4 Turn dough out onto a lightly floured work surface, and knead
several times.

5 Roll dough to ½" thickness. Cut into rounds with a 2" biscuit cutter.
Place on prepared pan, allowing 1" space between each.

6 Bake about 8 minutes, until tops are golden brown.

> **NOTE:** Serve warm with butter or as a base for Sullivan's crab
> cakes topped with Carolina rémoulade sauce.

> **CHEF'S TIP:** To make your own baking mix, combine 4½ cups
> all-purpose flour, 2 tablespoons baking powder, 1 tablespoon
> salt, 1 tablespoon sugar and 1 cup all-vegetable shortening,
> then process in a food processor until it becomes the texture
> of cornmeal. If you don't have a food processor, you can simply
> blend together using a handheld pastry blender. Store this
> baking mix airtight at room temperature up to 3 months. If you
> have the space to store it in the refrigerator, it will last up to
> 6 months.

Sweet Potato Biscuits

MAKES 12 MEDIUM or 24 petite biscuits

2½ cups all-purpose flour

2 tablespoons sugar

1 tablespoon baking powder

1½ teaspoons salt

½ cup cold butter, cut into small pieces

1 cup cooked, mashed sweet potato, room temperature

1 cup sour cream

1 Preheat oven to 425°F.

2 Lightly grease a cookie sheet.

3 Combine flour, sugar, baking powder and salt. Whisk together. Using a handheld pastry blender or food processor, cut butter into the dry ingredients until the butter is the size of peas.

4 Blend together the sweet potato and sour cream until smooth. Stir into the dry ingredients, just until the dough comes together; do not overmix.

5 On a lightly floured surface, knead the biscuit dough a few times. Roll dough to ¾" thick. Cut into rounds, and place 2" apart on prepared pan.

6 Bake 10–15 minutes until golden brown.

> **NOTE:** To turn these yummy Southern jewels into a more savory dish, add some minced fresh herbs, such as rosemary, sage or thyme, and serve with country ham, baked ham, breakfast sausage patties or pork tenderloin.

Whipping Cream Drop Biscuits

MAKES 12

2½ cups all-purpose flour

1 tablespoon baking powder

1 tablespoon granulated sugar

1 teaspoon salt

2 cups heavy whipping cream

1. Preheat oven to 425°F.

2. In a mixing bowl, combine dry ingredients, and stir to blend. Make a well in center of ingredients. Pour whipping cream into well. Stir just until the dough is well blended.

3. Onto a baking sheet, drop dough into 12 mounds of equal size, allowing about 2" in between.

4. Bake in center of oven for about 20 minutes, until tops of biscuits are light golden brown and bottoms are golden brown.

Strawberry Preserves
with Rose Geranium & Vanilla Essence

MAKES 8 JARS

This recipe is a favorite creation of mine. My mother is a purist and believes perfection (like traditional strawberry preserves) shouldn't be messed with. Well, the chef in me (or is it the rebel?!) screams out to try new things. I grow my own scented geraniums and use them to flavor these preserves. Also, I love to make scented sugars by placing the scented geranium leaves in sugar. Leave alone a month and then discard the leaves. Use the sugar in baked goods like sugar cookies and pound cakes. The taste is subtle but memorable.

8 half-pint canning jars, lids and screw-on bands

7 cups sugar

5 cups very thinly sliced, hulled ripe strawberries

8 rose-scented geranium leaves

1 teaspoon butter

1 (3-ounce) pouch liquid fruit pectin

2 teaspoons pure vanilla extract

1 Sterilize jars, lids and screw-on bands in boiling water for at least 5 minutes. Drain well just before filling jars with prepared preserves.

2 In a saucepan, combine sugar, strawberries, geranium leaves and butter (the little bit of butter helps reduce foaming). Bring to a boil, stirring often. Remove geranium leaves, and discard.

3 When you reach a rolling boil (one that you can't stir down), add pectin all at once. Stir well. Return to a boil, and boil exactly 1 minute. Remove from heat.

4 Stir in vanilla extract. Pour into hot, sterilized jars. Wipe rims of jars clean. Secure lids with screw-on bands.

5 Process jars of preserves in a boiling water bath for 10 minutes.

6 Carefully remove from water bath, and let stand at room temperature to cool.

7 In a few hours, check to be certain all jars are vacuum sealed. Store at room temperature up to 1 year. If you have a jar that didn't vacuum seal, refrigerate, and use within 1–2 weeks.

> **NOTE:** Rose geranium is a nonflowering plant found at a nursery, usually with the herbs. The leaves make this plant special because they are scented like roses. (There is also a lemon geranium variety.) You can also substitute 1 tablespoon food-safe rosewater.

Peach Cobbler Jam

MAKES 9 JARS

9 half-pint canning jars, lids and screw-on bands

7½ cups granulated white sugar

4 cups coarsely chopped peaches and their juice

¼ cup freshly squeezed lemon juice

2 tablespoons freshly grated gingerroot

1 tablespoon butter

1 teaspoon ground cinnamon

½ teaspoon freshly grated nutmeg

1 (3-ounce) pouch liquid fruit pectin

1 Sterilize jars, lids and screw-on bands in boiling water for at least 5 minutes. Drain well just before filling jars with prepared preserves.

2 In a large saucepan, combine everything but the pectin. Bring to a boil over medium heat, stirring often to keep from scorching.

3 When you reach a rolling boil (one that you can't stir down), add pectin all at once. Stir well. Return to a boil, and boil exactly 1 minute while stirring constantly. Remove from heat.

4 Pour into hot, sterilized jars. Wipe rims of jars clean. Secure lids with screw-on bands.

5 Place jars of preserves in a boiling water bath for 10 minutes.

6 Carefully remove from water bath, and let stand at room temperature to cool.

7 A couple of hours later, check to be certain all jars vacuum sealed. Leave undisturbed. It may take up to 2 weeks for the gel to completely set. Store at room temperature up to 1 year. If you have a jar that didn't vacuum seal, refrigerate, and use within 1–2 weeks.

Jingle Bell Candied Cranberries

MAKES 3 CUPS

1 pound washed fresh cranberries, picked through

2 cups granulated sugar

¼ cup high-quality bourbon

1 Preheat oven to 350°F.

2 Fully line the interior of a jelly-roll pan with foil. Spray with nonstick spray. Scatter cranberries in pan.

3 Sprinkle evenly with sugar. Cover tightly with foil.

4 Bake 1 hour. Remove from oven, and drizzle bourbon over cranberries. Let stand 10 minutes. Transfer to a bowl. Store tightly covered in the refrigerator.

> NOTE: Don't you just love it when a recipe has so many uses?! These candied cranberries are truly special and enhance so many dishes. Serve this dish simply as your holiday dinner cranberry dish. Then think of the other ways to enjoy these spiked, candied bits of bliss: as a topping for mixed green salads with blue cheese dressing, with a variety of fine cheeses and crackers, as a topping for baked brie, scattered over roasted poultry...

Southern Christmas Ambrosia

SERVES 12

SALAD

6 oranges, peeled, cut into sections, or 2 large cans mandarin orange sections, drained well

1 fresh pineapple, peeled, cored, cut into 1" chunks

1 cup red seedless grapes, cut in half

2 apples, cored, cut into 1" chunks

1 cup coarsely chopped pecans

1 (6-ounce) package frozen coconut, thawed

½ cup golden raisins or dried cranberries

½ cup thinly sliced celery

DRESSING

2 cups sour cream

½ cup golden or cream sherry

1 packed cup light brown sugar

Salad

Combine all salad ingredients, and toss well.

Dressing

Combine all dressing ingredients, and stir until sugar dissolves. Pour dressing over salad. Stir gently. Cover, and refrigerate at least 4 hours or up to 2 days before serving.

Uptown Down-South Cheese Grits

SERVES 8–10

½ gallon milk

¼ cup butter

2 teaspoons salt

2 cups grits

1 cup whipping cream

6 ounces (1½ cups) grated smoked Gouda cheese

Tabasco sauce to taste

1 In a large saucepan, combine milk, butter and salt. Bring to a boil over medium-high heat.

2 Whisk in grits. Continue to whisk 1 minute more. Reduce heat, cover, and simmer until grits are tender and liquid has been absorbed. Whisk or stir often to discourage lumps and prevent sticking.

3 Add whipping cream, and stir to blend.

4 Stir in cheese, and blend well. Season to taste with Tabasco sauce and additional salt, if needed.

Mama Cruz's Recipe File

When Helen, Maddie and I decided to open *The Corner Spa*, not a one of us knew a thing about proper exercise or working out. Oh, we'd take a jab at jogging from time to time or lifting an occasional weight over at Dexter's gym, but we were far from being experts. Truth be told, we weren't all that enthusiastic about exercise. That's when we decided we'd better hire personal trainer Elliott Cruz as an independent contractor to run the fitness side of our business.

I'd like to tell you we made that decision based solely on his résumé, which was rock-solid, but it was his equally rock-solid abs that really won us over. That man could be the poster boy for fitness! I swear, half the women who joined the spa did so just so they could watch him giving lessons. Even our seniors take a weekly jazzercise class just to ogle him and make the sort of smart remarks that make him blush. I'm not kidding! They'll tell you that themselves. Helen's mother, Flo Decatur, is the leader of this outrageous pack.

Still, it was mostly a business relationship (honest!) until Elliott started romancing Karen Ames, a struggling single mom who worked for me at Sullivan's. Then we all discovered the man could cook, and everything he'd learned in the kitchen, he'd learned from his mamacita, Maria Cruz.

As I understand it, Mama Cruz has always kept a tightfisted grip on her recipe secrets, using them as leverage to guarantee that all her children and their families show up every week for Sunday dinner. Karen says her mother-in-law has always sworn she'd take her blend of peppers and spices for her incredible mole sauce to the grave with her just to be sure they come visit the cemetery in the hope she'll communicate it from the great beyond. Somehow, though, Karen managed to wrestle it away from her to include here. Just wait till you taste Mama Cruz's enchilada casserole with classic mole sauce.

Elliott's the one who forked over the seafood paella recipe, a meal that makes good use of all the fresh Lowcountry seafood we have available around here. Add a salad and a nice white wine, and you have the makings for a fabulous party!

Since she's been married to a man who definitely likes a little spice in his life and in his food, Karen's taken to doing her own experimenting here in the Sullivan's kitchen, stealing a page right out of Mama Cruz's book. Her jalapeño mac and cheese has become a local favorite…and it's been quite a boon for our beverage sales, too! First Elliott and now his wife can't seem to go anywhere without generating plenty of heat.

Though I'm all about Southern cooking with a twist at Sullivan's, personally there's nothing I'd like better than having more specialties from other countries available right here in Serenity. When I was growing up, pizza and spaghetti were about as adventurous as we got. A Chinese take-out place opened a few years ago. Now that I've sampled a few of Mama Cruz's specialties, I'm thinking there ought to be an authentic Mexican restaurant here in town. Maybe Karen and I should talk about whether her mother-in-law would be open to starting a new restaurant with us. I'm always ready for new business opportunities. Try these recipes, and see what you think.

Dulce De Leche Cheesecake Bars

MAKES 24

CRUST

1¼ cups finely crushed Mexican "Maria"cookies, vanilla wafers or graham crackers

½ cup butter, melted

FILLING

1 (8-ounce) package cream cheese, softened

1 cup sugar

3 eggs, room temperature

1 tablespoon vanilla extract

½ teaspoon salt

1 (14-ounce) can dulce de leche

Crust

1 Preheat oven to 350°F.

2 Grease a 13" x 9" x 2" baking pan.

3 Combine ingredients and press into bottom of prepared pan. Bake 15 minutes. While crust is baking, prepare filling.

Filling

1 Cream together cream cheese and sugar. Beat in eggs.

2 Stir in vanilla and salt, then spread the mixture on the hot baked crust.

3 Heat dulce de leche until very hot and melted, then drizzle it over cheesecake layer. Using a skewer or the tip of a knife, swirl dulce de leche into cheesecake layer.

4 Cover pan tightly with foil and place in a large roasting pan. Add boiling water to roasting pan until water comes halfway up the sides of the baking pan. Bake 1 hour.

5 Remove from oven. Carefully lift pan out of water bath and place on a cooling rack, then remove the foil. Let cool to room temperature.

6 Cover and store in the refrigerator until ready to serve. Cut into 24 squares.

Chicken Enchilada Casserole
with Speedy Mole Sauce

SERVES 6–8

CASSEROLE

6 boneless, skinless chicken breast halves (about 2¼ pounds total)

1 envelope dry taco seasoning

2 tablespoons vegetable or canola oil

12 ounces shredded Mexican cheese blend

1 (15-ounce) can black beans, rinsed, drained well

1 (15-ounce) can whole-kernel corn, drained well

10 (6-inch) corn tortillas

1½ cups sour cream

SAUCE

1 large medium-diced sweet onion

2 tablespoons vegetable or canola oil

3 tablespoons cocoa powder

1 envelope dry taco seasoning

2 (10¾-ounce) cans tomato soup concentrate

2 (10-ounce) cans mild RO·TEL tomatoes

1 milk chocolate Hershey's bar (no nuts)

GARNISHES (OPTIONAL)

Finely diced fresh jalapeño peppers

Minced fresh cilantro

Sour cream

Guacamole

Casserole

1 Place chicken breast halves on a plate. Sprinkle both sides of each breast with taco seasoning.

2 In a skillet over medium heat, heat oil until hot but not smoking. Add chicken breast halves to skillet. Brown chicken on both sides, turning halfway through cooking, for a total cooking time of about 10 minutes.

3 Remove chicken from pan, and let stand 5 minutes before cutting into thin slices.

Sauce

1 Sauté onion in oil until crisp tender. Add cocoa powder and taco seasoning.

2 Stir together tomato soup and tomatoes. Add to the sauce, and blend well.

3 Cook over medium heat 5 minutes, stirring often.

4 Remove from heat, and crumble chocolate bar over top. Let stand for several minutes, then stir melted chocolate into the sauce.

Assembly

1 Preheat oven to 350°F.

2 Grease a 13" × 9" × 2" baking pan.

3 Combine half of the sauce with the thinly sliced chicken breasts. Add half of the cheese blend along with the black beans and corn. Stir to combine.

4 Spoon half of the remaining sauce in the bottom of the prepared pan. Set aside remaining sauce.

5 Divide chicken mixture among the 10 tortillas. Roll tightly.

6 Crowd the filled enchiladas in the pan on top of the sauce. Spoon all remaining sauce over top. Drop sour cream in dollops over the sauce.

7 Cover tightly with foil, and place in center of oven. Bake 40 minutes.

8 Remove casserole from oven, and remove foil. Raise oven temperature to 400°F. Scatter remaining cheese over top of casserole. Return casserole to oven, and cook an additional 10 minutes, until cheese melts and begins to brown.

To Serve

Remove casserole from oven, and let stand at least 5 minutes before serving with desired garnishes.

Jacked-Up Tex-Mex Macaroni & Cheese

SERVES 6–8

1 pound breakfast sausage

1 cup chopped onion

1 envelope taco seasoning

1 (14-ounce) can spicy RO·TEL tomatoes

1 cup sour cream

1 pound elbow macaroni, cooked in salted water until al dente, drained well

8 ounces grated cheddar cheese

8 ounces grated Monterey Jack cheese

4 cups milk

6 large eggs, beaten

Salsa of your choice

1 Preheat oven to 350°F.

2 Generously grease a 13" × 9" × 2" baking dish or other suitable casserole dish.

3 In a large skillet over medium-high heat, cook sausage, stirring to crumble.

4 Add onion and taco seasoning. Cook until onion is softened. Remove from heat, and stir in tomatoes and sour cream. Set aside.

5 In bottom of prepared dish, distribute half of the macaroni. Evenly spoon on half of the meat and then half of each cheese. Repeat layering once more.

6 Whisk together milk and eggs. Slowly pour over entire casserole contents.

7 Cover tightly with foil, and bake 45 minutes. Remove foil, and bake an additional 15–20 minutes, until cheese is melted and top is golden brown.

8 Remove from oven, and let stand 7–10 minutes before serving. Serve with salsa.

Pico de Gallo

MAKES 2 CUPS

7 finely chopped jalapeño peppers, ribs and seeds removed

3 Roma tomatoes, seeded, diced

1 small white onion, finely chopped

¼ cup minced fresh cilantro

Juice of 1 lime

Salt to taste

Combine all ingredients, and stir to blend. Cover, and refrigerate up to 1 week.

> **NOTE:** Brace yourself because this is one brazen pico! Fresh jalapeño peppers have so much flavor. By removing the seeds and ribs from these peppers, about 70% of their heat is removed. If you like this pico hotter still, leave in some of the seeds and ribs.

Smoky Pork-Filled Tamales

SERVES 6–8

1 (8-ounce) package dried corn husks

FILLING

1 (1¼ pounds) pork tenderloin

2 cups large-diced onion

3 garlic cloves, roughly chopped

1 (12-ounce) can beer

SAUCE

1 dried ancho chili pepper

1 tablespoon vegetable oil

1 tablespoon flour

½ cup cooking liquid from pork

1 tablespoon smoked paprika

1 garlic clove, minced

1 teaspoon red wine vinegar

1 teaspoon ground cumin

1 teaspoon fresh oregano or
½ teaspoon dried

½ teaspoon crushed red pepper flakes

Seasoned salt to taste

TAMALE DOUGH

1 cup lard

1 teaspoon salt

3 cups masa harina

1½ cups cooking liquid from pork

Husks

Place corn husks in a large bowl. Cover with hot water, and let soak about 3 hours (while the pork filling cooks). Use a dinner plate to help keep the corn husks submerged in the water.

Filling

1 Place pork tenderloin, onion and garlic in a large pot. Add beer and enough water to cover tenderloin. Bring to a boil.

2 As soon as water boils, reduce heat to simmer, and cover pot with a lid. Simmer at least 3 hours, until pork is tender.

3 When pork is done, remove from pot, reserving 1½ cups of the cooking liquid. Once the pork is cool enough to handle, shred the pork using two forks, then coarsely chop.

Sauce

1 Toast the ancho in a skillet over medium-high heat. Keep a close eye on the pepper so it doesn't burn. Remove from heat, and let cool until you can handle it.

2 Remove the stem and seeds from the ancho. Crumble and grind in a clean coffee grinder or with a mortar and pestle.

3 Heat oil in a medium saucepan over medium heat. Add flour, and cook until the mixture has browned somewhat and begins to smell nutty.

4 Add ½ cup cooking liquid from pork, stirring until smooth. Add ground ancho and remaining sauce ingredients.

5 Reduce heat to simmer, and add shredded pork. Cover with lid, and let simmer 30 minutes.

Tamales

1 Using an electric mixer on high speed, blend together lard and salt until light and fluffy.

2 Add masa harina in several additions, and blend at low speed until fully incorporated.

3 Add remaining pork cooking liquid, a little at a time, enough to form a spreadable dough, similar to a soft cookie dough.

4 Remove the corn husks from their soaking water. Working with 1 tamale at a time, flatten out a corn husk. Have the narrow end facing you. Place a dollop (about 2 tablespoons) of dough in center of corn husk. Leaving an outer margin of about ⅓ the husk, spread dough to cover the remaining husk.

5 Spread a heaping tablespoon of pork filling down the center of the tamale. Roll up the corn husk, starting at one of the long sides. Fold the narrow end of the husk onto the rolled tamale, and secure with kitchen twine.

6 Layer tamales in a steamer basket. Steam over boiling water 1 hour. Add water to the steamer as needed during the cooking time.

> **NOTE:** It's true love and indeed a labor of love when Mama Cruz makes tamales. She normally triples the recipe to feed the crowd. Any leftovers (yeah, right!) can be stored covered in the refrigerator up to 3 days, then steamed again to reheat.

Southern Seafood Paella

SERVES 6–8

4½ cups chicken broth

1 (10-ounce) bottle clam juice

¾ cup white port or dry sherry

2 star anise (do not omit this seasoning)

2 teaspoons sea salt

1 teaspoon smoked paprika

¾ teaspoon crushed red pepper flakes

½ teaspoon saffron threads

1 pound arborio rice

4 tablespoons extra-virgin olive oil

2 large onions, cut into medium dice

4 ounces Spanish chorizo sausage, casing removed, thinly sliced

3 ounces country ham, trimmed, cut into small dice

3 ounces smoked bacon, cut into thin strips

4 garlic cloves, minced

4 ounces fresh green beans, trimmed, cut into 1" pieces

¾ cup frozen peas

10 large sea scallops, cut in half

12 ounces grouper, cut into 1" chunks

18 raw jumbo shrimp, shelled, deveined

1 pound live mussels, scrubbed, beards removed

1 (10-ounce) jar roasted red peppers, drained, cut into strips

1 lemon, thinly sliced

½ cup minced fresh parsley

For sanity's sake, have all ingredients prepped and ready before starting this dish.

1 In a medium saucepan, combine first 8 ingredients to make stock. Bring to a boil, then lower heat to a simmer, and cook at least 15 minutes. Remove star anise from broth. Meanwhile, proceed with recipe.

2 Rinse rice under running water until water runs clear. In a standard (12") paella pan or heavy-bottomed skillet of similar size, heat olive oil until hot but not smoking over medium-high heat. Sauté onions until crisp tender.

3 Add chorizo, country ham and bacon. Cook 2–3 minutes.

4 Stir in garlic, and sauté briefly.

5 Add drained rice, green beans and peas; stir to coat with oil.

6 Add seasoned stock to the rice mixture. Bring to a boil, stirring constantly. Reduce heat to low, and simmer for 15 minutes, cooking uncovered and without stirring.

7 Cover pan with lid or foil, and cook 5 minutes more. Most of the liquid should now be absorbed. If not, cover, and cook an additional 5 minutes.

8 Arrange all of the seafood on top, ending with the shrimp and mussels. Re-cover, and let simmer for an additional 5 minutes, or until the shrimp turns pink, the mussels open, and all liquid has been absorbed. Discard any mussels that do not open.

9 Arrange the red pepper strips and lemon slices over the top. Sprinkle with parsley, and serve immediately.

> **NOTE:** Don't let the long list of ingredients scare you away from this recipe—it is heavenly! This classic Spanish dish gets all gussied up Southern style. The intense flavors, vibrant colors and festive presentation are a feast for the eyes as well as the palate. This is truly special-occasion fare at its finest!

Black Bean Chili

SERVES 6

1 pound ground pork breakfast sausage

1½ cups diced onion

1 tablespoon minced garlic

1 envelope taco seasoning

1 tablespoon dried oregano

1 teaspoon ground cumin

3 cups water

3 (15-ounce) cans black beans, rinsed well, drained

1 (15-ounce) can diced tomatoes

1 (15-ounce) can crushed tomatoes

1 tablespoon red wine vinegar

1 In a large soup pot, brown the sausage over medium-high heat, stirring to crumble.

2 Add onion, and cook until crisp tender.

3 Add garlic, and cook 1 minute before adding the taco seasoning, oregano and cumin.

4 Add the remaining ingredients. Bring to a boil, then lower heat, cover pot, and let simmer at least 15 minutes.

> **NOTE:** Can you keep a secret? Mama Cruz sure can! This is her quick-and-easy—but oh, so tasty—recipe for a super yummy and hearty black bean chili. The flavors are so well balanced and complex that you would swear she had been slaving over a hot stove all day. In truth, it can be made and served in about half an hour—start to finish! Another great thing about this chili is that the ingredients can be easily doubled (or tripled!) to suit your size gathering. Any leftovers freeze well.

Roasted Corn & Mixed Bean Salsa

SERVES 8–10

3 ears corn, shucked, silks removed

1 (15-ounce) can black beans, rinsed, drained

1 (15-ounce) can small red beans, rinsed, drained

3 green onions, minced

1 bell pepper, seeded, diced

2 jalapeño peppers, minced (remove seeds and ribs for milder salsa)

1 cup diced tomato

½ cup balsamic vinaigrette

¼ cup minced cilantro

2 garlic cloves, minced

Salt and pepper to taste

Grill corn on all sides until done. Remove from grill to cool. Cut kernels from cob. Combine with remaining ingredients. Chill thoroughly. Serve with tortilla chips.

CAUTION: Wear plastic gloves when working with hot peppers, and avoid contact with face.

Tex-Mex Appetizer Cheesecake

SERVES 16

CRUST

1½ cups crushed Ritz crackers

¼ cup melted butter

FILLING

2 (8-ounce) packages cream cheese, softened

3 large eggs, beaten

1 envelope taco seasoning

1 (4-ounce) can diced green chili or chipotle peppers, drained well

1 (4-ounce) jar diced pimentos, drained well

8 ounces (2 cups) shredded Mexican cheese blend

1 cup sour cream

GARNISHES (OPTIONAL)

Salsa

Guacamole

Corn chips

Crust

Preheat oven to 325°F. Spray a 9" springform pan with cooking spray. Stir together cracker crumbs and butter. Press firmly into the bottom of the pan. Bake 15 minutes.

Filling

1 In a medium mixing bowl, blend together the cream cheese and eggs until smooth.

2 Stir in taco seasoning, peppers and pimentos. Add the shredded cheese, and stir just until incorporated. Pour mixture over baked crust.

3 Bake 30 minutes.

4 Remove from oven. Immediately spread sour cream over cheesecake. Cool to room temperature. Cover, and refrigerate at least 4 hours or up to several days before serving.

5 Release cheesecake from pan. Slice into wedges, and top with your favorite salsa and/or guacamole. Serve with sturdy corn chips.

Tres Leches Cake

SERVES 12

CAKE

6 large eggs, separated

2 cups granulated sugar

2 cups all-purpose flour

2 teaspoons baking powder

¾ teaspoon salt

½ cup whole milk

1 teaspoon vanilla extract

SOAKING LIQUID

1 (14-ounce) can sweetened condensed milk

1 (14-ounce) can evaporated milk

1 cup heavy whipping cream

TOPPING

2 cups heavy whipping cream

¼ cup sugar

1 teaspoon pure vanilla extract

GARNISH

1 pound fresh strawberries, sliced or cut in half

Cake

1 Preheat oven to 350°F.

2 Lightly grease and flour a 13" × 9" × 2" baking pan.

3 Using an electric mixer, beat egg whites until frothy. Add sugar gradually, beating all the while, until stiff peaks form. Add egg yolks, 1 at a time, beating well after each addition.

4 Whisk together flour, baking powder and salt.

5 Add the flour mixture to the batter alternately with the milk, beginning and ending with the flour mixture. Stir in vanilla extract.

6 Transfer the batter to the prepared pan, and spread the batter level. Bake about 25 minutes, until golden and tester inserted in center comes out clean.

7 Remove from oven, and place on a cooling rack. Pierce cake all over with a wooden skewer.

Soaking Liquid

Whisk together the soaking liquid ingredients, but do not incorporate any air into the liquid. Pour mixture over the hot cake in several additions, letting each soak in before adding more. When all the liquid has been absorbed, cover with plastic food wrap, and refrigerate at least 6 hours or up to 3 days before serving.

Topping

Combine all topping ingredients in a large mixing bowl. Using an electric mixer, beat on high speed until stiff peaks form. Spread over top surface of cake.

Garnish

Arrange strawberries on cake or on each individual serving.

Chef Erik's
Decadent Desserts

When I hired Erik Whitney straight out of the Atlanta Culinary Institute as my pastry chef here at Sullivan's, I suspected he wouldn't stay in Serenity for long. He was a big city guy through and through, an ex-paramedic who'd gone to culinary school after his wife died. He'd done it mostly to shake himself out of his grief. I think he was as shocked as anyone when it became his career destiny.

Despite his claim that he'd found his niche in the world, I figured he'd tire of cooking, grow weary of small-town life or, because he's absolutely fantastic, be hired away by some fancy gourmet restaurant over in Charleston. Believe me, any one of those things could have happened, but I hadn't taken into account the impact my friend Helen would have on him.

It seems the uptight, control-freak lawyer had finally met her match, the one man on Earth who wouldn't take any of her nonsense and trampled right on over her defenses. I claimed an emergency and begged her to help out in the kitchen at Sullivan's more than once just to watch the fireworks between those two! They kept Maddie and me entertained for months as they fought the attraction. They're now happily married and the parents of the most adorable little girl you've ever seen. Feisty little Sarah Beth, the perfect blending of their strong-willed personalities, is going to give them headaches when she hits her teens, I guarantee it.

Though Erik's my sous-chef now, he still specializes in pastry. Believe me, there's no one in these parts who does it better. I'm just waiting for the day when a customer comes in, skips right over the main courses that are my personal pride and joy and goes straight to the dessert menu and orders everything!

Who could resist that traditional Southern favorite, a moist red velvet cake with a frosting that melts in sugary, buttery heaven on the tongue? Then there's the personal favorite of some of my friends, Erik's baked apple bread pudding with homemade cinnamon ice cream and caramel sauce. One of our standbys that's always a hit is the warm walnut brownie, served à la mode with hot fudge sauce. It takes an easy treat and turns it into something divine.

Since I've had my issues with a family history of diabetes, every now and again I push for desserts that even I can eat without guilt. Erik created his no-sugar-added chocolate amaretto cake just for me. Trust me, it makes up for needing to steer clear of some of those other options. Well, maybe not the bread pudding. I've always had a fondness for that. It's something my grandma used to make, though hers couldn't hold a candle to Erik's.

And because I need to watch my sugar intake, here's a little tip I've learned about dessert. Sometimes just a taste or two is enough.

I'm looking into experimenting with those tiny dessert samplers served in some restaurants, no more than a couple of bites in a two-ounce shot glass. I like to call them desserts without guilt or temptation. I figure there aren't enough calories or sugar to throw most diets into a tailspin. And since there's no great big dessert sitting on a plate to tempt you to eat more than you should, well, it just makes life easier.

I'll bet your guests would appreciate that, too. Think about those portion sizes next time you have folks over, and remember that sometimes a little can go a long way when it comes to sweet, heavenly decadence!

Pluff Mud Fudgy Bottom Peanut Butter Icebox Pie

SERVES 6–8

FUDGE

½ cup heavy whipping cream

6 ounces semisweet chocolate chips

CRUST

1 (6-ounce) prepared chocolate cookie crumb crust

FILLING

8 ounces cream cheese

1 cup granulated sugar

1 tablespoon vanilla extract

1 cup creamy peanut butter

1 cup heavy whipping cream, whipped firm

6 coarsely chopped regular-size Reese's peanut butter cups

GARNISHES (OPTIONAL)

Whipped cream

Chopped peanuts

Chopped Reese's peanut butter cups

Chocolate or caramel sauce

Fudge

1 Heat whipping cream until almost boiling. Remove from heat.

2 Stir in chocolate chips. Cover, and let stand 5 minutes.

3 Whisk until smooth. Spoon ¾ cup into bottom of pie crust, and set aside.

4 Cover, and refrigerate the remaining chocolate sauce. It will be used at serving time as a topping.

Filling

1 In a mixing bowl, combine cream cheese, sugar and vanilla. Beat until smooth.

2 Beat in peanut butter.

3 Stir in whipping cream until no white streaks appear.

4 Stir in Reese's cups.

5 Spoon into crust over chocolate layer. Cover, and refrigerate (or freeze!).

To Serve

Place a wedge of pie in center of dessert plate. Heat remaining fudge until hot and liquid. Spoon or drizzle over pie. Then, top with any desired toppings.

> **NOTE:** What's not to like here?! Because this dessert is so rich (like cheesecake!), small servings are a must. If you choose to freeze the pie, just remove from freezer 30 minutes before slicing and serving. Yummy!

Southern Supreme Red Velvet Cake

SERVES 16–20

CAKE

1½ cups granulated sugar

½ cup shortening

1 teaspoon vanilla

2 eggs

2 tablespoons cocoa powder

2 ounces red food coloring

2½ cups all-purpose flour

1 teaspoon salt

1 cup buttermilk

1 tablespoon white vinegar

1 teaspoon baking soda

ICING

1¼ cups milk

6 tablespoons flour

1½ cups granulated sugar

1 cup butter, room temperature

1 teaspoon pure vanilla extract

Cake

1 Preheat oven to 350°F.

2 Grease and flour two 9" round cake pans.

3 In a large mixing bowl, using an electric mixer, cream together sugar, shortening and vanilla. Add eggs, 1 at a time.

4 Make a paste by stirring together cocoa and food coloring. Add to the creamed mixture.

5 Sift together flour and salt. Add alternately with buttermilk to batter, beginning and ending with flour.

6 Combine vinegar and baking soda. Stir into batter.

7 Divide batter evenly between prepared pans. Firmly rap cake pans on countertop to level batter.

8 Bake 30–35 minutes or until a cake tester inserted in center comes out clean. Prepare frosting.

9 Cool in pans 10 minutes on rack. Remove from pans. Cool thoroughly.

10 Split cake layers in half horizontally, making 4 layers total.

Icing

1 Whisk together milk and flour. Pour through a wire mesh strainer (to remove any lumps) into a medium saucepan. Add sugar to the saucepan.

2 Cook mixture over medium heat, stirring constantly, until the mixture thickens and begins to boil. Continue to stir and cook for 2 minutes.

3 Remove from heat and transfer mixture to a mixing bowl. Place in refrigerator about one hour, stirring mixture several times during the cooling period. (Cool mixture to approximately 70°F.)

4 Using an electric mixer, blend the cooled flour/milk/sugar mixture with the room temperature butter. Add vanilla. Beat until light and fluffy, scraping down the bowl several times while beating.

Assemble

Spread ¼ of the icing between each layer and on the top of the cake. Do not frost sides of cake. Store covered in the refrigerator (or at room temperature during colder months).

NOTE: This is one of Chef Erik's signature desserts. The icing is just so ethereal, so light and fluffy. If, however, you prefer a cream cheese frosting with your red velvet cake, by all means...

Buttermilk-Glazed Carrot Cake
with Orange Cream Cheese Frosting

SERVES 16–20

CAKE

2 cups all-purpose flour

2 teaspoons baking soda

2 teaspoons ground cinnamon

½ teaspoon salt

2 cups sugar

¾ cup vegetable oil

¾ cup buttermilk

3 eggs, beaten

2 teaspoons pure vanilla extract

2 cups grated carrots

1 (8-ounce) can crushed pineapple, drained well

1 cup chopped walnuts

1 (3½-ounce) can flaked coconut

GLAZE

1 cup sugar

½ cup buttermilk

½ cup butter

1 tablespoon light corn syrup

½ teaspoon baking soda

1 teaspoon pure vanilla extract

FROSTING

12 ounces cream cheese, softened

¾ cup butter, softened

3 cups sifted confectioners' sugar

1 tablespoon orange juice concentrate, thawed

1½ teaspoons vanilla extract

1½ teaspoons freshly grated orange zest

Cake

1 Preheat oven to 350°F.

2 Grease and flour two 9" round cake pans.

3 Sift together flour, baking soda, cinnamon and salt.

4 In a large mixing bowl, combine sugar, oil, buttermilk, eggs and vanilla. Beat 2 minutes at medium speed using an electric mixer.

5 Add flour mixture, and blend. Stir in remaining ingredients.

6 Pour batter into prepared pans. Bake 35–40 minutes or until wooden pick inserted in center comes out clean.

7 Remove from oven, and place pans on cooling rack.

Glaze

1 Combine all ingredients except vanilla in a small saucepan. Bring to a boil, and cook 5 minutes, stirring often.

2 Remove from heat, and stir in vanilla.

3 Spread over cakes while cakes are still hot. Cool in pans 15 minutes.

4 Carefully remove from pans, and let layers cool completely.

Frosting

1 Using an electric mixer, blend together cream cheese and butter.

2 Add remaining ingredients, and beat until smooth. You may need to refrigerate icing to firm and reach desired spreadable consistency.

3 Spread between cake layers and on the sides and top.

4 Cover, and refrigerate up to 4 days before serving.

Coconut Cream Tart in Pecan Shortbread Crust

SERVES 8

CRUST

3 cups pecan sandie cookie crumbs (the size of bread crumbs or slightly more coarse)

½ cup confectioners' sugar

½ cup melted butter

FILLING

1 (15-ounce) container whole-milk ricotta cheese

1 (8-ounce) package cream cheese, softened

1 (4-serving) package coconut instant pudding

1 cup cream of coconut (such as Coco Lopez)

1 cup sifted confectioners' sugar

1 (3½-ounce) can coconut, divided

Crust

Combine crust ingredients, and mix well. Spoon mixture into a 9–10" tart pan with removable bottom. Press mixture firmly and evenly up sides and in bottom of pan. Refrigerate to firm up and fill later, or proceed.

Filling

In a medium mixing bowl, combine all ingredients except canned coconut. Beat with an electric mixer until mixture is smooth and creamy. Stir in ⅔ can of coconut. Spoon filling into tart shell, and sprinkle on remaining coconut. Refrigerate until serving time.

Southern Cream Cheese Pound Cake

SERVES 16–20

3 cups granulated sugar

1 (8-ounce) package cream cheese

1 cup (2 sticks) butter (not margarine)

6 large eggs

3 cups lightly measured cake flour

1 tablespoon pure vanilla extract

1 tablespoon pure almond extract

Finely grated zest of 1 lemon

> **NOTE:** 1 hour before making pound cake, remove butter, cream cheese and eggs from refrigerator, and let stand at room temperature for only 1 hour.

1 Preheat oven to 325°F.

2 Using a bit of butter and flour, grease and flour either a 12-cup 1-piece tube pan or a 12-cup Bundt pan.

3 In a large bowl, using an electric mixer on medium speed or a standing mixer on medium-low speed, cream together sugar, cream cheese and butter. Blend about 5 minutes.

4 Add eggs, 1 at a time, blending well after each addition.

5 Sift flour 3 times. Add flour in 3 additions to batter, scraping sides and bottom of bowl after each addition. Do not beat batter. Blend just briefly until all flour is incorporated.

6 Stir in extracts and lemon zest.

7 Pour batter into pan. Drop pan onto countertop to level batter and to help remove any air bubbles.

8 Place in center of oven, and bake about 90 minutes, until wooden pick or cake tester inserted into center comes out clean.

9 Remove from oven, and place pan on cooling rack. Let cool 10 minutes.

10 Remove cake from pan, and place on cooling rack. Let cake cool thoroughly. Slice and serve. Store airtight at room temperature.

Cinnamon Roll Bread Pudding

with Whipped Vanilla Bean Crème

SERVES 8–10

BREAD PUDDING

2 (11½-ounce) packages store-bought cinnamon rolls with icing

1 quart half-and-half, heated until very warm

1¾ cups sugar, divided

½ cup melted butter

4 eggs, beaten

1 tablespoon pure vanilla extract

½ teaspoon salt

TOPPING

1 (8-ounce) package cream cheese, softened to room temperature

½ cup sugar

1 vanilla bean

1½ cups cold heavy whipping cream

Bread Pudding

1. Preheat oven to 350°F.
2. Grease a 13" × 9" × 2" baking dish.
3. Tear cinnamon rolls into 1" chunks, and set aside.
4. In a large mixing bowl, combine half-and-half, 1½ cups sugar and remaining ingredients. Blend well.
5. Add torn cinnamon rolls, and stir to blend.
6. Pour mixture into prepared pan. Cover tightly with foil, and bake 45 minutes.
7. Remove foil. Sprinkle top with remaining ¼ cup sugar. Return to oven, and bake an additional 15 minutes.

> **NOTE:** Reheats easily in the microwave.

Topping

In a small mixing bowl, beat cream cheese and sugar until sugar is dissolved. Split vanilla bean in half lengthwise. Remove seeds from the inside by scraping with the tip of a knife. Place vanilla bean seeds in with cream cheese and sugar. Add whipping cream slowly, and using an electric mixer, blend on high speed until medium-firm peaks form. Serve on each individual serving of bread pudding.

> **NOTE:** You'll flip over the simplicity of this dessert, and do back-flips over the taste!!

Baked Apple Bread Pudding

with Cinnamon Ice Cream & Caramel Sauce

SERVES 12

BREAD PUDDING

1 (10-ounce) loaf stale French bread, thinly sliced

3 cups sugar

3 cups half-and-half

4 eggs, beaten

½ cup melted butter

1 tablespoon pure vanilla extract

1 teaspoon ground cinnamon

½ teaspoon freshly grated nutmeg

1 (20-ounce) can apple pie filling

ICE CREAM

½ gallon vanilla bean ice cream

2 teaspoons ground cinnamon

SAUCE

1 firmly packed cup light brown sugar

½ cup dark corn syrup

6 tablespoons unsalted butter

1½ cups heavy whipping cream

1 teaspoon pure vanilla extract

Bread Pudding

1 Preheat oven to 350°F.

2 Generously grease a 13" × 9" × 2" baking pan.

3 Tear bread into pieces, and set aside.

4 Combine sugar, half-and-half, eggs and butter. Beat well.

5 Stir in vanilla, cinnamon and nutmeg. Add apple pie filling and bread pieces. Blend well.

6 Pour into prepared pan. Cover tightly with foil, and bake 1 hour.

7 Remove foil. Return to oven, and bake an additional 15–20 minutes, or until knife inserted in center comes out clean.

8 Cool briefly before serving. Serve alone or topped with cinnamon ice cream and warm caramel sauce.

Ice Cream

Remove ice cream from freezer, and let stand at room temperature 5–10 minutes. Stir in cinnamon. Return to freezer to firm up.

Sauce

1 In a large, heavy saucepan, stir together brown sugar, corn syrup and butter. Cook over medium heat, stirring often, until butter and sugar are melted and the mixture is smooth.

2 Add whipping cream and vanilla. Increase heat to high, and bring to a boil. Continue to boil until caramel is somewhat reduced and reaches 225°F. **Makes 2½ pints.**

Pumpkin Cake Roll

SERVES 8–10

CAKE

3 eggs

1 cup sugar

¾ cup firmly packed canned pumpkin

¾ cup all-purpose flour

2 tablespoons finely minced crystallized ginger

2 teaspoons ground cinnamon

1 teaspoon baking powder

1 teaspoon ground nutmeg

½ cup chopped pecans

Confectioners' sugar

FILLING

1 (8-ounce) package cream cheese, softened

1 cup confectioners' sugar

4 tablespoons butter, softened

1 teaspoon vanilla

Cake

1 Preheat oven to 375°F.

2 Grease 15" × 10" × 1" jelly-roll pan. Line bottom with wax paper or parchment.

3 Using an electric mixer, beat eggs on high speed 5 minutes. Add sugar very gradually, beating until thick. Fold in pumpkin.

4 Combine all dry ingredients except pecans and sugar. Fold into batter.

5 Pour into pan, and spread evenly. Sprinkle with chopped pecans. Bake 12–15 minutes.

6 Sift confectioners' sugar liberally over a kitchen towel. Turn cake out onto towel. Carefully peel off parchment. Using a pizza wheel, trim away edges. Cool on rack 10 minutes.

7 Starting at one of the short sides, roll cake up, towel and all, while cake is still warm. Place seam-side down on cooling rack. Cool thoroughly.

Filling

Combine all ingredients, and beat until light and fluffy. Carefully unroll cake. Spread with filling. Roll up, peeling away towel from cake as it rolls. Wrap roll securely in plastic wrap. Place seam-side down on tray. Refrigerate several hours or up to 3 days. Freezes well up to 1 month.

To Serve

Remove plastic wrap, and place seam-side down on serving platter. Sprinkle with confectioners' sugar. Serve with slightly sweetened whipped cream and a dusting of nutmeg, if desired.

Chocolate Sugarplum Truffles

MAKES ABOUT 4 DOZEN

1½ cups heavy whipping cream

¼ cup high-quality cognac

2 (12-ounce) bags semisweet chocolate chips

½ cup coarsely chopped dried, sweetened cranberries

¼ cup finely chopped dried apricots

¼ cup dried currants

European-processed cocoa powder

1 In a microwave-safe dish, combine whipping cream and cognac. Heat just to a boil.

2 Remove from microwave, and stir in chocolate. Let stand 5 minutes.

3 Whisk until melted and smooth. Stir in dried fruits. Cool to room temperature.

4 Cover, and refrigerate until firm.

5 Shape into 1" balls, and roll in cocoa. Cover, and refrigerate up to 1 month.

> **NOTE:** This recipe calls for you to roll the prepared truffle in cocoa powder. If you prefer your truffles to have a hard chocolate shell, you can freeze the truffles first, then dip the frozen truffles, one at a time, into melted chocolate. Let harden completely before storing airtight.

Deep-Dish Apple Pie
with Crunchy Crumb Topping

SERVES 6–8

CRUST

1½ cups all-purpose flour

5 tablespoons shortening or lard

4 tablespoons butter, cut into cubes

½ teaspoon salt

3 tablespoons ice water

FILLING

5 cups very thinly sliced, peeled, cored Granny Smith apples

¼ cup flour

½ packed cup light brown sugar

½ cup granulated sugar

1½ teaspoons apple pie spice

TOPPING

¾ cup flour

⅓ cup sugar

½ cup butter, softened

> **NOTE:** This recipe includes a no-fail pie crust!

Crust

1 At least 30 minutes before making the pie crust, combine the first 4 ingredients in the bowl of a food processor fitted with the metal blade, and chill for at least 30 minutes. (This cold method ensures a flaky crust.)

2 When the ingredients are cold, place the bowl on the food processor, and pulse a few times to incorporate the ingredients.

3 With the machine running, add the water through the top of the machine. Do not overwork the dough. Process it just until the dough becomes quite crumbly and does not gather up into a ball in the food processor.

4 Gather the dough into a ball with your hands. You may squeeze the dough to help it stay together. If it still won't form a ball, you can add a tiny bit more ice water. Shape the ball into a flat disc. Wrap in plastic food wrap, and refrigerate at least 30 minutes.

5 On a cool, lightly floured surface, roll dough out to fit your deep-dish pie plate. Transfer dough, and fit into the pie plate, turning edges under and crimping the rim of the crust.

Filling

Preheat oven to 350°F. Toss the apple slices with the flour. Add sugars and apple pie spice to the apples. Transfer mixture to the pie crust.

Topping

Using your hands, combine the flour and sugar. Work in the butter until you have large clumps. Distribute evenly over the apple filling.

Pie

Place pie in center of oven. Bake about 1 hour, covering top of pie with foil if the crust edge and/or crumb topping seems to be browning too quickly. Remove from oven, and let cool for at least 30 minutes before slicing.

Valentine's Special Decadence Cake

Flourless Chocolate Cake

SERVES 12

CAKE

¾ cup butter, cut into small pieces

1 (12-ounce) bag semisweet chocolate chips

6 large eggs, separated

12 tablespoons sugar, divided

2 teaspoons pure vanilla extract

GLAZE

½ cup heavy whipping cream

½ cup dark corn syrup

1 (12-ounce) bag semisweet chocolate chips

Cake

1 Preheat oven to 350°F.

2 Grease a 9" springform pan. Line bottom with parchment or wax paper. Wrap entire outside of pan with heavy-duty foil.

3 Melt butter, and bring to a boil.

4 Place chocolate chips in a medium mixing bowl. Pour hot butter over chocolate, and let stand 5 minutes. Stir until smooth.

5 Using an electric mixer, beat egg yolks and 6 tablespoons sugar in a large bowl until mixture is thick and pale, about 3 minutes.

6 Add chocolate mixture and vanilla to yolk mixture. Stir until smooth.

7 Using clean, dry beaters, beat egg whites in a large bowl until soft peaks form. Gradually add remaining 6 tablespoons sugar, beating until stiff. Fold into chocolate mixture in 3 additions.

8 Pour batter into prepared pan. Bake 1 hour. Cake top will be puffed and cracked when done.

9 Cool cake in pan on cooling rack 15 minutes. Cake will fall.

10 Using a spatula or the back of a large spoon, press edges of cake to be level with the center. Leave cake in pan until thoroughly cooled.

11 Run thin knife around inside edge to loosen cake. Remove wall of springform pan. Invert cake onto a 9" cardboard round. Peel off parchment.

Glaze

1 In a medium saucepan, bring cream and corn syrup to a boil.

2 Remove from heat, and add chocolate. Let rest 5 minutes.

3 Gently stir until smooth; you do not want to create any air bubbles in the glaze.

4 Cover a work surface with parchment or foil. In the center of your prepared work surface, elevate the cake (on the cardboard round) by placing it on top of a bowl smaller than the cardboard round.

5 Spread 1 cup glaze over cake top. Pour glaze over cake sides. Using an icing spatula, scrape up glaze that has dripped onto parchment to reuse. Repeat glazing the cake top and sides until almost all glaze is used. Wipe clean the bottom rim of cardboard round. Place cake on a platter, and chill at least 1 hour or until glaze is firm. Can be made up to 3 days ahead.

To Serve

Serve with lightly sweetened, freshly whipped cream or fresh berries. Add garnish if desired.

Garnish (Optional)

Pour a few ounces of melted chocolate into a freezer-strength zip-top bag. Snip a tiny hole in corner of bag. On parchment or waxed paper, drizzle chocolate into desired shapes. (I think a heart shape is romantic.) Let chocolate harden. Carefully peel away from parchment. Or make chocolate curls and sprinkle with confectioners' sugar.

> **NOTE:** Beware, chocoholics—you may have met your match here!!

Warm Walnut Brownie à la Mode

with Hot Fudge Sauce

SERVES 12

BROWNIE

2 cups sugar

1½ cups all-purpose flour

¾ cup cocoa powder

1 teaspoon salt

1 cup melted butter, cooled a bit

5 eggs, beaten

1 teaspoon vanilla

1½ cups chopped walnuts

6 ounces semisweet chocolate chips

HOT FUDGE SAUCE

⅓ cup heavy whipping cream

⅓ cup light corn syrup

6 ounces semisweet chocolate chips

Brownie

1 Preheat oven to 350°F.

2 Grease a 13" × 9" × 2" baking pan.

3 In a large mixing bowl, combine first 4 ingredients.

4 Whisk together butter, eggs and vanilla. Add wet ingredients to dry ingredients, and stir. Do not overmix. Add walnuts and chocolate chips.

5 Pour batter into prepared pan. Spread batter level. Bake 30 minutes.

6 Cool 30 minutes before slicing and serving with ice cream and hot fudge sauce. Store airtight up to 2 days.

Hot Fudge Sauce

In a microwave-safe bowl, combine whipping cream and corn syrup. Cook on high power until mixture comes to a boil. Add chocolate chips, and let stand at room temperature 5 minutes. Whisk until smooth. Serve warm over anything that could stand a deep, rich chocolate sauce. This keeps for up to 6 months covered in the refrigerator and can be reheated.

Candied Orange Peel

MAKES ABOUT 6 CUPS

6 large oranges

Cold water

3 cups granulated sugar, divided

1 Wash oranges. Using an orange peeler or knife, score orange into quarters. Remove orange peel, keeping peel intact. (Save oranges for another use.) Slice peel diagonally into thin strips.

2 Place in a large saucepan or Dutch oven. Fill pot ¾ full with cold water. Bring to a boil, and boil for 1 minute. Drain oranges.

3 Return orange peel to pot, and repeat procedure 4 more times. (This removes the bitterness from the peel.) Have ready baking sheets lined with paper towels.

4 Bring 2 cups granulated sugar and 1 cup water to a boil, stirring until sugar is dissolved.

5 Add drained orange peel to syrup. Cook orange peel in syrup about 10 minutes, stirring constantly. The peel will absorb most of the syrup.

6 Drain off any remaining syrup. Using tongs, transfer candied orange peel to prepared baking sheets, arranging in single layers and allowing a bit of space between each piece. Dry at room temperature at least 4 hours.

7 Coat candied peel in remaining 1 cup granulated sugar, shaking off excess. Store airtight at room temperature up to 1 week or in the freezer up to 2 months. Use in recipes calling for candied orange peel.

> **NOTE:** Although time consuming, this recipe isn't hard to make and is well worth the effort. For a special Christmas treat, take the candied peel (but not sugar coated), and dip the pieces in melted dark chocolate. After letting the chocolate harden on the candied peel, store airtight at room temperature for up to 1 month.

Southern Pecan Toffee

SERVES 20

1 stack saltine crackers

1 cup unsalted butter

1 packed cup brown sugar

1 cup chopped pecans

1 (8-ounce) bag brickle bits (Heath bar toffee chips)

1 (12-ounce) bag milk chocolate chips

1 Preheat oven to 375°F.

2 Completely line the interior of a 15" × 10" × 1" jelly-roll pan with aluminum foil. Smooth out all wrinkles, and spray with nonstick cooking spray. Place saltines in pan side by side.

3 In a medium saucepan, melt butter. Stir in brown sugar and pecans. Bring to a boil. Stirring occasionally, let mixture boil 5 minutes only.

4 Remove from heat. Pour mixture over saltines. Bake 10 minutes.

5 Remove from oven, and place on cooling rack. Immediately sprinkle half the bag of brickle bits over hot toffee. Evenly distribute chocolate chips over hot toffee. Let stand several minutes.

6 Using an off-set spatula, spread chocolate over toffee. Immediately sprinkle remaining brickle bits over melted chocolate. Cover tightly with foil, and let cool until firm. (**Note:** You can speed this up by placing in the refrigerator; just make sure that it is tightly covered with foil so it doesn't pick up any humidity.)

7 Remove from refrigerator, and break into pieces like peanut brittle. Store airtight at room temperature.

> **WARNING:** This stuff has to be as addictive as any substance ever imagined. There surely is a support group out there somewhere whose members, although anonymous, all have melted chocolate in the corners of their mouths and bits of toffee stuck in their back teeth!

Chocolate Amaretto Cake

No Sugar Added

SERVES 12

CAKE

1 cup milk

½ cup canola or vegetable oil

2 large eggs

1 teaspoon pure almond extract

1 teaspoon pure vanilla extract

2¼ cups baking Splenda

1¾ cups all-purpose flour

¾ cup cocoa powder

1 teaspoon salt

½ teaspoon baking powder

½ teaspoon baking soda

½ cup boiling water

½ cup amaretto

TOPPING

¾ cup thinly sliced almonds

1 cup heavy whipping cream

2 tablespoons baking Splenda

½ teaspoon pure almond extract

Cake

1 Preheat oven to 350°F.

2 Grease and flour two 8" round cake pans.

3 In a mixing bowl, combine milk, oil, eggs and extracts. Blend together.

4 In a separate bowl, whisk together Splenda, flour, cocoa, salt, baking powder and baking soda. Add to the wet ingredients.

5 Using an electric mixer, beat on medium speed for 2 minutes.

6 Combine boiling water and amaretto. Add slowly to batter, and blend thoroughly. Batter will be very thin.

7 Divide batter evenly between the two cake pans. Bake 10 minutes.

8 Turn cake layers out of pans onto cooling racks. Let cool thoroughly.

Topping

After the cake layers come out of the oven, scatter the almonds on a baking sheet, and bake at 350°F about 8 minutes, until lightly browned and almonds begin to smell toasted. Set aside to cool. In a medium mixing bowl, combine whipping cream, Splenda and almond extract. Beat on high speed until firm peaks hold.

To Serve

Cut cake layers into wedges or chunks. Place cake on dessert plates. Top with the whipped cream and toasted almonds.

The Corner Spa's Low-Cal Healthy Selections

When Maddie was going through her divorce, tensions were running pretty high among the Sweet Magnolias. I'd been divorced from Ronnie for a while, but I knew better than anyone that what Maddie really needed was a challenge. Not that being a single mom to three children isn't difficult enough, but Helen and I knew Maddie needed to get her legs back under her. What she needed most of all was a boost to her self-esteem.

And what we all needed was a pleasant place to exercise. I mean, it's not as if a one of us could work up any enthusiasm for the treadmill in the first place, but at least it needed to be located someplace that wasn't a dump. Dexter's gym was all Serenity had, and sweet as he is, Dexter had let the place get so run-down, only the desperate would go there for a workout.

What Serenity needed—or at least what the women in town needed—was a place not only to get fit but to be pampered too. The minute the idea came to me and Helen, we were all over it, but Maddie took a whole lot of convincing, especially since she had only sweat equity to contribute. I think once she realized how difficult it was going to be to create a business plan, deal with renovations and get the doors open, she started feeling a whole lot better about her contribution. She was, after all, putting in the hard work. All Helen and I did was give her a budget to work with. She made The Corner Spa the success it is today, and she did it practically single-handedly, which not only assured us a healthy bottom line but also gave her self-esteem just the boost it needed.

Despite all the credit that belongs to Maddie, I'd like to think at least part of The Corner Spa's success is due to the little café we created so women could take a break after working out or getting a massage or mani-pedi. Of course, the menu had to be healthy. And since we weren't going to have a kitchen on the premises, it had to be simple, special things that could be prepared fresh at Sullivan's each day or easily blended right on the premises.

Our smoothies are one of the most popular items we serve. Who wouldn't enjoy sitting under a big ol' shade tree on our brick patio with a tropical fruit smoothie after a hard workout? Or how about a bowl of spicy, chilled gazpacho? Talk about refreshing!

Because every woman tends to feel incredibly virtuous after an hour or so of exercise, there's no reason to spoil that mood with something heavy. Our low-fat chunky apple muffins with a glass of tea seem faintly decadent, but they won't break the calorie bank.

My personal favorite for the woman who needs to grab something quick on the go after using her lunch hour to work out is our chicken Caesar salad wrap. It's low-calorie and filling but light enough that it won't ruin that high that comes from putting in some time on the treadmill.

In fact, that's what all the recipes in this section are about: healthy eating, whether it's after a workout or just an alternative on a hot summer evening. And these just go to prove that tasty doesn't have to be loaded down with fat!

Corner Spa Tortilla Soup

SERVES 8–10

8 ounces boneless, skinless chicken breasts, cubed

2 cups frozen whole-kernel corn, thawed

2 (14½-ounce) cans fat-free chicken broth (low-sodium preferred)

1 (10¾-ounce) can tomato puree

1 (10-ounce) can diced tomatoes and green chilies

1 large onion, chopped

2–3 garlic cloves, pressed or minced

1 tablespoon sugar

2 teaspoons ham base or bouillon

2 teaspoons ground cumin

1 teaspoon chili powder

⅛–¼ teaspoon cayenne pepper

2 bay leaves

4 (5½") corn tortillas

GARNISHES (OPTIONAL)

Chopped fresh cilantro

Fat-free or low-fat sour cream

> **NOTE:** This recipe can be prepared in a slow cooker or on the stovetop.

Slow Cooker

Combine all ingredients except the tortillas in a 4-quart slow cooker. Cover, and cook on high 6–8 hours.

Stovetop

Combine all ingredients except the tortillas in a Dutch oven, and bring to a boil over medium-high heat, stirring occasionally. Reduce heat to low, and simmer 1 hour minimum.

1 Preheat oven to 375°F.

2 Remove and discard bay leaves.

3 Cut tortillas into ¼"-wide strips, and place on baking sheet. Bake 5 minutes.

4 Stir and rearrange tortillas on baking sheet. Bake additional 5 minutes or just until crisp.

5 Ladle soup into soup bowls. Sprinkle tops with crispy tortilla strips, and garnishes.

Summer Gazpacho

SERVES 8

2 large vine-ripe tomatoes or 6 Roma tomatoes, peeled

1 cucumber, peeled, seeded

½ bell pepper, seeded

½ cup fresh parsley

1 (46-ounce) can tomato juice

¼ cup extra-virgin olive oil

¼ up red wine vinegar

1 tablespoon Worcestershire sauce

½ teaspoon Tabasco sauce

Salt and pepper to taste

1 lemon, thinly sliced

1 cup sour cream

GARNISH (OPTIONAL)

Minced cilantro or parsley sprigs

1 Place tomatoes, cucumber, bell pepper and parsley in a food processor or blender, and process until finely minced.

2 Add tomato juice, olive oil, vinegar, Worcestershire sauce, Tabasco, salt and pepper, and stir to combine well.

3 Add lemon slices, and stir into soup.

4 Refrigerate, and allow flavors to develop several hours until mixture is thoroughly chilled.

To Serve

Ladle into chilled soup bowls, and place a dollop of sour cream on top. Garnish with minced cilantro or additional parsley.

Vidalia Onion Vinaigrette

MAKES 2½ CUPS

1 large Vidalia onion or other sweet onion

½ cup white wine Worcestershire sauce

½ cup water

¼ cup honey

2 tablespoons coarse-grain Dijon mustard

Celery salt and freshly ground black pepper to taste

Combine all ingredients in container of food processor or blender. Blend until smooth. Cover, and refrigerate up to 1 week.

Corner Spa Cream of Carrot Soup

SERVES 6

2 cups chicken or vegetable stock

1 pound carrots, peeled, thinly sliced

1 medium onion, diced

1 cup sliced celery

2 tablespoons minced fresh mint or
2 teaspoons dried, crushed

2 cups soy milk

1 teaspoon MAGGI liquid seasoning*

Salt and pepper to taste

GARNISHES (OPTIONAL)

Sour cream

Minced fresh mint

In a Dutch oven, combine the first 5 ingredients. Bring to a boil over high heat. Cook until vegetables are tender. Using a blender, puree mixture (in batches if necessary). Combine pureed mixture with soy milk. Heat through. Season with MAGGI seasoning, salt and pepper. Garnish with a drizzle of sour cream and minced fresh mint.

* Note: MAGGI liquid seasoning can be easily found in the soup aisle of most grocery stores.

Cucumber Cooler

MAKES ABOUT 3 QUARTS

1 cucumber, peeled, seeded, coarsely grated

1 quart cold water

1 (1-liter) bottle chilled lemon-lime soda

1 (1-liter) bottle seltzer or sparkling water

GARNISHES (OPTIONAL)

Thin cucumber slices

Lemon slices

Lime slices

In a pitcher, combine grated cucumber and water. Cover, and refrigerate at least 2 hours or up to 24 hours before serving. Strain, and discard cucumber. When ready to serve, combine cucumber essence water with remaining ingredients. Serve in tall glasses over crushed ice. Garnish with cucumber, lemon and lime slices.

> **NOTE:** Talk about refreshing—this cooler is a girl's best friend after a good workout at The Corner Spa.

Southern Legacy Apple & Mint Spritzer

No Sugar Added

MAKES ABOUT 1 GALLON

4 cups water

1 packed cup mint leaves

Grated zest from 1 lime

4 cups apple juice

Freshly squeezed juice of 1 lime

1 (2-liter) bottle diet lemon-lime soda, chilled

GARNISHES (OPTIONAL)

Lime slices

Apple wedges

Mint sprigs

Bring water to a boil. Remove from heat. Add mint and lime zest. Cover and let steep at least 30 minutes. Strain, and discard lime zest and mint. Cool the flavored water. When ready to serve, combine the flavored water with the remaining ingredients. Serve in tall glasses over ice. Garnish with lime slices, apple wedges and mint sprigs.

Fuzzy Navel Smoothie

SERVES 2

1 (6-ounce) container fat-free, no-sugar-added peach yogurt

1 cup frozen peach slices

1 cup freshly squeezed orange juice

Place all ingredients in a blender. Process until smooth. Serve immediately.

Chunky Apple Bran Muffins

Low-Fat

MAKES 12

1½ cups wheat bran

1 cup low-fat buttermilk

1 cup all-purpose flour

½ packed cup brown sugar

1 teaspoon cinnamon

1 teaspoon baking soda

½ teaspoon salt

2 egg whites

1 teaspoon pure vanilla extract

2 medium apples, cored, medium diced

1 Preheat oven to 350°F. Line a 12-cup muffin tin with paper liners, or use a nonstick cooking spray.

2 Whisk together wheat bran and buttermilk. Set aside to soak for 10 minutes.

3 In a mixing bowl, mix together flour, brown sugar, cinnamon, baking soda and salt. Whisk egg whites and vanilla into the bran mixture.

4 Combine the wet and dry mixtures, and blend briefly. Stir in the apples by hand.

5 Divide batter among the muffin cups. Bake 18–20 minutes, until a pick inserted in center comes out clean.

Almond Biscotti

MAKES 3 DOZEN

¾ cup sugar

½ cup butter, softened

2 eggs, beaten

2 teaspoons almond extract

2½ cups all-purpose flour

1 tablespoon baking powder

¾ teaspoon salt

⅔ cup coarsely chopped toasted almonds

Milk

1 Preheat oven to 350°F.

2 Line cookie sheet with nonstick aluminum foil or parchment.

3 In a large mixing bowl, using an electric mixer, cream sugar and butter until light and fluffy.

4 Add eggs and almond extract. Mix well.

5 Combine dry ingredients except nuts, and add to dough. Dough will be very stiff. Stir in nuts by hand.

6 With floured hands, divide dough in half. Shape each half into a log measuring 14" × 3". Place logs, several inches apart, on prepared cookie sheet. Smooth the top of each. Brush with milk, then sprinkle with additional sugar.

7 Bake 25–30 minutes, until golden brown.

8 Remove from oven. Reduce oven temperature to 300°F.

9 Carefully transfer loaves to cooling rack. Cool 10 minutes.

10 Carefully transfer to cutting board. Using assertive force, slice on the diagonal into ¾" slices.

11 Place upright on baking sheet, allowing a bit of space between pieces. Bake at reduced temperature 20 minutes (to dry out biscotti).

12 Remove from oven, and transfer to cooling racks. Cool thoroughly. Store airtight up to 1 month. Freezes beautifully.

> **NOTE:** These Italian twice-baked cookies are simple to make. They're a bit time consuming but well worth the effort. They are best enjoyed with a cup of coffee, cappuccino, hot tea, port or dessert wine. Go ahead and dunk them. Although the little old genteel ladies of Charleston might not agree, it's well accepted to do so.

Chicken Caesar Salad Wraps

1 pound boneless, skinless chicken breast halves

1 tablespoon garlic salt

1 tablespoon minced fresh rosemary

1 teaspoon freshly ground black pepper

1 large head romaine lettuce, torn into bite-size pieces

1 cup low-fat garlic croutons

1 cup homemade or store-bought Caesar salad dressing

6 (8") flour tortillas

½ cup freshly grated Parmesan cheese

GARNISHES (OPTIONAL)

Fresh fruit

Celery slices

Thinly sliced carrots

1 Rinse and pat dry chicken. Lay side by side on a surface lined with paper towels.

2 Blend together garlic salt, rosemary and pepper. Evenly divide among the chicken breasts, and rub into the chicken.

3 In a large skillet over medium-high heat, cook chicken breasts about 10 minutes, turning halfway through cooking. Chicken is thoroughly cooked at 165°F. (Every cook should have at least 1 instant-read thermometer.)

4 Remove chicken from skillet, and let cool to room temperature.

5 Once cooled, cut chicken into very thin strips. Combine with lettuce, croutons and salad dressing.

6 On a clean kitchen work surface, lay tortillas side by side. Divide the salad mixture among the tortillas. Sprinkle Parmesan over the salad. Wrap each sandwich like a burrito. Wrap in parchment paper, and refrigerate up to 8 hours before serving.

To Serve

Leaving the parchment paper wrapping on the sandwich, cut sandwich in half diagonally. Serve with a fresh fruit garnish and a few pieces of celery and thinly sliced carrots.

Mixed Salad

with Strawberry & Basil Vinaigrette

SERVES 6–8

VINAIGRETTE

1 cup sliced strawberries

4 packets Splenda

⅓ cup white balsamic vinegar

2 tablespoons minced fresh basil
or 2 teaspoons dried

1 cup vegetable oil

Salt and freshly ground black pepper
to taste

SALAD

Mixture of baby lettuces and crisp
lettuce (such as red leaf, romaine
or Bibb)

1 red onion, very thinly sliced and
separated into rings

GARNISH (OPTIONAL)

Caramelized almonds

Vinaigrette

In food processor or blender, combine strawberries and their juice,
along with Splenda, with vinegar and basil. With machine running,
add oil in a thin, steady stream. Process 1 minute more. Season with
salt and pepper to taste.

Salad

Combine ingredients, and serve with strawberry vinaigrette and
caramelized almonds.

Balsamic Vinaigrette

Fat-Free

MAKES 2 CUPS

2 teaspoons cornstarch

1 cup water

¾ cup balsamic vinegar

¼ cup orange marmalade

¼ cup dried minced onion

1 tablespoon minced fresh garlic

1 tablespoon minced fresh basil

2 teaspoons seasoned salt

1½ teaspoons minced fresh thyme or ½ teaspoon dried

1½ teaspoons minced fresh oregano or ½ teaspoon dried

½ teaspoon freshly ground black pepper

1 bay leaf

Dissolve cornstarch in water. In a blender, combine dissolved cornstarch with remaining ingredients except bay leaf. Process until smooth. Transfer to a small saucepan, and add bay leaf. Bring to a boil over medium heat, stirring occasionally. Remove from heat, and cool thoroughly. Remove bay leaf. Cover, and refrigerate up to 1 month.

Gold Nugget Chicken & Pasta Salad

SERVES 8

SALAD

3 pounds boneless, skinless grilled chicken breasts, cut into chunks

8 ounces whole-grain rotini pasta, cooked according to package directions, drained well

1½ cups thinly sliced celery

½ cup finely diced fresh pineapple

½ cup chopped dried papaya

½ cup chopped dried mango

½ cup golden raisins

DRESSING

1 cup low-fat mayonnaise

2 teaspoons curry powder

Salt and freshly ground black pepper to taste

GARNISH

1 cup roasted, salted cashew halves

In a large mixing bowl, combine all salad ingredients. Whisk together the dressing ingredients. Spoon dressing over salad, and stir well to blend. Cover, and refrigerate at least 4 hours or up to 4 days before serving. Garnish each serving with a sprinkling of cashew halves.

Holidays &
Get-Togethers

In Serenity, there's nothing we love more than our holiday celebrations and community events. Whether it's the annual Fourth of July parade with its accompanying hoopla, backyard barbecues and fireworks, our fall festival or Christmas with Santa on the town green, we'll use any excuse to gather and celebrate.

The Sweet Magnolias are no different. Not every gathering is a margarita night. We bring our whole families together for everything, from birthday parties to cookouts at the drop of a hat, just the way I'm sure you do with your friends and neighbors. If you don't, then start making time for these relaxing get-togethers.

With so many of us these days, along with our growing number of children and grandchildren, it's quite a crowd. We dole out assignments, and everyone brings along a specialty, made in quantities large enough to feed a lot of people. Some things are traditional, and we simply couldn't have a party without them.

It's gotten to be a huge joke around town that no Serenity Christmas tree-lighting ceremony would be complete without eggnog. Believe you me, that raised a few eyebrows at first, especially with newcomers to Serenity, but we serve an alcohol-free version that suits the town's holiday spirit just fine. It makes our police chief and town manager happier, too.

Right after the annual Fourth of July parade, no barbecue at my place would be complete without front porch sippin' lemonade. There's nothing better on a hot summer day, and around these parts you can just about guarantee there will be heat and humidity on the Fourth. After watching all the former members of the armed forces, elaborate floats and bands march through town, that lemonade is the perfect antidote to being parched. It also gives us just enough refreshing oomph to pay a visit to all the vendors who come to town for the occasion before we settle down with our burgers, hot dogs and potato salad.

Usually we like to stick to the traditional barbecue on the Fourth, but at least once during the summer we get together for a backyard Lowcountry seafood boil. Oh, my! All that fresh, succulent seafood just reminds us how blessed we are to live in this area. Now you'll be able to try it wherever you are.

Whenever we're getting together, just us Sweet Magnolias, for a baby or wedding shower, for instance, we like to pull out all the stops and do something a little special. The amaretto and pecan baked brie makes eyes light up. The last time we were together, I made Erik's grilled cheese panini with a pecan-pesto mayonnaise and spicy tomato jam. Once you've tried it, you'll never look at a plain old grilled cheese sandwich the same way again. I guarantee it.

And, of course, no New Year's celebration down South would be complete without hoppin' John New Year's salad. They say it brings luck throughout the whole year. I can't swear there's any truth to that, but I do know that the Sweet Magnolias have had more than our share of luck over the years. Oh, we've had our trials and disappointments, but I'd have to say we've faced them all with courage and grace. And, most important of all, of course, we've not once faced them alone.

Down here in Serenity, we like to set a table loaded down with incredible food whenever we get together. It's a key ingredient to the Southern hospitality on which we all pride ourselves. But, if you ask me, the most important ingredient of all is friendship. With a glass of sweet tea or a margarita and a friend by your side, there's not a thing in the world that can keep you down for long! Try it, and see if that's not so.

Christmas Festival Eggnog

Alcohol-Free

MAKES 1 GALLON

4 cups whole milk

8 whole cloves

2 (3") cinnamon sticks

1 whole nutmeg, broken into bits using a rolling pin or meat mallet

12 egg yolks

1⅔ cups sugar, divided

4 cups half-and-half

1 tablespoon rum extract

2 cups heavy whipping cream

1 teaspoon pure vanilla extract

½ teaspoon freshly grated nutmeg

1 Combine milk, cloves, cinnamon sticks and nutmeg in a large saucepan. Cook over medium-low heat, stirring often. Bring to a low boil.

2 In a large bowl, combine egg yolks and 1⅓ cups sugar. Beat together until fluffy.

3 Whisk the hot milk mixture into the egg yolk mixture very slowly.

4 Return mixture to the saucepan. Cook over medium heat 3–5 minutes, stirring constantly until mixture thickens. Do not allow mixture to boil.

5 Strain mixture through a fine-wire mesh strainer. Let cool at least 1 hour.

6 Stir in half-and-half and rum extract. Cover, and refrigerate until thoroughly chilled or up to 4 days before serving.

7 Just before serving, beat together heavy cream, remaining ⅓ cup sugar and vanilla until soft peaks form.

8 Pour eggnog into a small punch bowl. Drop whipped cream into the mixture in dollops, then fold into the eggnog. Add freshly grated nutmeg to float on top.

Poinsettia Punch

MAKES 1 GALLON

2 (12-ounce) bags frozen raspberries, thawed

1 (12-ounce) can frozen pink lemonade concentrate, thawed

½ cup sugar

1 (750-milliliter) bottle white zinfandel wine, chilled

1 (2-liter) bottle raspberry-flavored or regular ginger ale, chilled

In a food processor, blend together raspberries, lemonade concentrate and sugar. Process 1 minute. Pour mixture through a wire mesh strainer, pressing mixture against the sides of the strainer. Discard seeds. Refrigerate raspberry mixture until thoroughly chilled. When ready to serve, blend with wine and ginger ale.

> **NOTE:** This gorgeous punch has a low alcohol content and is the perfect choice when you want to serve up just a little holiday "spirit." You may also leave out the wine totally, replacing it with an equal amount of cran-raspberry juice cocktail.

Golden Wassail

MAKES ABOUT 5 QUARTS

½ gallon apple cider

1 (46-ounce) can pineapple juice

2 (12-ounce) cans apricot nectar

4 cups water

1 cup sugar

1 (6-ounce) can frozen orange juice concentrate, thawed

1 (6-ounce) can frozen lemonade concentrate, thawed

24 whole cloves

6 (3") cinnamon sticks

In a Dutch oven, combine all ingredients. Bring to a boil. Reduce heat, cover, and simmer 45 minutes to 1 hour. Strain, and discard spices. Serve hot. Refrigerate up to 2 weeks.

White Sangria

MAKES 5 QUARTS

1 (2-liter) bottle lemon-lime soda, chilled

1 (750-milliliter) bottle white wine, chilled

2 (12-ounce) cans guanabana nectar (found in Mexican food section in grocery stores and in Mexican markets)

1 (12-ounce) can frozen lemonade concentrate, thawed

1 (12-ounce) can frozen limeade concentrate, thawed

1 (10-ounce) can frozen piña colada drink mix, thawed

1–2 cups vodka (you decide!)

GARNISHES (OPTIONAL)

Lemon slices

Lime slices

Fresh pineapple chunks

Combine all ingredients, and serve cold with lemon, lime and pineapple.

NOTE: Don't you just love sangria?! This is not your ordinary sangria. Because it is light in color, it makes a beautiful presentation in a pitcher or punch bowl with all the lemon and lime slices and chunks of fresh pineapple. It's great for sipping the summer away. Make a nonalcoholic version for the kids simply by replacing the wine and vodka with more lemon-lime soda.

Front Porch Sippin' Lemonade

MAKES 2 QUARTS

2 pounds lemons, washed

2 cups boiling water

1½ cups sugar

Cold water

1 Using a vegetable peeler, remove zest from lemons. Add lemon zest to boiling water. Cover, and let steep 30 minutes.

2 Remove and discard lemon zest. Add sugar to warm lemon water. Stir to dissolve. Let lemon syrup cool to room temperature.

3 Transfer lemon syrup to a 2-quart pitcher.

4 Cut lemons in half, and squeeze out their juice. This should yield about 1½ cups freshly squeezed lemon juice. Stir lemon juice into the lemon syrup.

5 Add enough cold water to equal 8 cups lemonade. Stir well. Refrigerate until serving time. Serve in tall glasses with lots of ice.

> **NOTE:** This recipe makes one smooth but strong lemonade—perfect for leisurely afternoons and front porch sippin'. The melting ice will not dilute it too much. For an adult libation, add a jigger of your favorite gin to each glass.

Iced Almond-Lemonade Tea

MAKES 1 GALLON

8 cups boiling water

4 family-size iced tea bags

1 cup sugar

1 (12-ounce) can frozen lemonade
concentrate, thawed

1 tablespoon pure almond extract

Cold water

Pour boiling water over tea bags, and let steep 5–10 minutes. Remove and discard tea bags. Add sugar, and stir until dissolved. Stir in lemonade concentrate and almond extract. Add enough cold water to measure 1 gallon.

Hot Cocoa

SERVES 4–6

½ cup sugar

⅓ cup unsweetened dark cocoa powder (European style/Dutch processed)

½ teaspoon salt

4 cups whole milk

1½ cups heavy whipping cream

GARNISHES (OPTIONAL)

Freshly whipped cream

Marshmallows

In a blender or food processor, thoroughly combine sugar, cocoa powder and salt. Transfer to a medium saucepan. Slowly whisk in milk and whipping cream until smooth. Heat over medium heat, stirring often, until very hot but not boiling. Ladle into mugs, and serve topped with freshly whipped cream or marshmallows (preferably homemade— see next recipe).

> **NOTE:** This is fabulous cocoa—sure to chase away the winter blahs. Feel free to add a bit of your favorite liqueur, such as amaretto, Grand Marnier, framboise, Frangelico or peppermint schnapps. Yummy!!

Homemade Marshmallows

MAKES 60 MEDIUM MARSHMALLOWS

4 envelopes unflavored gelatin

1½ cups water, divided

3 cups sugar

1¼ cups light corn syrup

¼ teaspoon salt

1 teaspoon pure almond extract

1 teaspoon pure vanilla extract

1 pound confectioners' sugar

1 Lightly oil a 13" × 9" × 2" baking dish. Line with foil, and smooth out all wrinkles. Generously oil the foil. Coat the oiled foil with a generous sprinkling of confectioners' sugar.

2 In the bowl of an electric mixer, soften the gelatin in ¾ cup water.

3 In a heavy saucepan, combine the remaining ¾ cup water, sugar, corn syrup and salt. Bring to a boil, and cook over high heat until the syrup reaches 234–240°F on a candy thermometer.

4 Remove from heat. Stir in the extracts.

5 With the whisk attachment of the mixer at full speed, add the hot syrup in a thin, steady stream to the softened gelatin. Beat at highest speed at least 5 minutes, until very thick and full volume.

6 Pour mixture into prepared pan. Let rest uncovered 10–12 hours at room temperature.

7 Sift a layer of confectioners' sugar on a large cutting board. Turn stiffened marshmallow mixture onto sugar. (**Note:** If marshmallow sticks to foil, lift marshmallow on foil from pan. Trim edges, and peel foil from marshmallow.)

8 Using oiled cookie cutters or a knife, cut into desired shapes. Coat all cut surfaces of marshmallows in confectioners' sugar to prevent sticking. Store airtight at room temperature up to 2 weeks.

Crabgrass

SERVES 12-16 as a hearty appetizer.

2 (10-ounce) packages frozen chopped spinach

¼ cup butter

1½ cups chopped mild onions

1 pound lump crabmeat, picked over

1 (8-ounce) package cream cheese, softened

1 cup sour cream

1½ cups freshly grated Parmesan cheese

⅛ teaspoon cayenne pepper

1 Thaw spinach, drain, and squeeze dry.

2 In a skillet, melt butter, and sauté onions about 4–5 minutes.

3 Add spinach, and sauté another 2–3 minutes.

4 Add the remaining ingredients. Heat through, and serve in a chafing dish with crackers or melba toast rounds.

> **NOTE:** This is also a great spread to fill a hollowed-out bread round. Wrap tightly with foil, and bake at 350°F for 30–40 minutes. Serve with torn pieces of bread for dipping.

Mulled Wine Punch

MAKES 1 GALLON

½ gallon apple cider

2 (750-milliliter) bottles dry red wine

2 cups water

½ cup honey

4 (3") cinnamon sticks

1 teaspoon whole cloves

1 teaspoon whole allspice

In a Dutch oven, combine all ingredients. Bring to a boil over high heat. Reduce heat, and simmer 15–20 minutes. Strain, and discard spices. Serve hot.

Spicy Pickled Shrimp

SERVES 12

½ cup cane or malt vinegar

¼ cup Creole mustard

3 tablespoons sugar

1 tablespoon OLD BAY Seasoning

1 teaspoon cayenne pepper

1 cup extra-virgin olive oil

1 cup diced onion

1 cup green onions, thinly sliced
on the diagonal

1 chopped bunch fresh parsley

1 tablespoon minced garlic

2 pounds cooked, peeled, deveined
large or extra-large shrimp

In a blender or food processor, combine first 5 ingredients. With
machine running, add oil in a thin, steady stream. Combine remaining
ingredients in a large glass bowl. Pour dressing over all. Stir well.
Refrigerate at least 12 hours or up to 3 days before serving.

Orange & Toasted Pecan Appetizer Torte

SERVES 30 as an appetizer spread.

FIRST LAYER

2 (8-ounce) packages cream cheese, softened

2 tablespoons mustard-mayonnaise sauce

8 ounces (2 cups) shredded sharp cheddar cheese

1 (7-ounce can) crushed pineapple, drained

½ cup chopped green onions

2 teaspoons dried mint

1½ cups chopped pecans, toasted

SECOND LAYER

2 (8-ounce) packages cream cheese, softened

¾ cup orange marmalade

1 tablespoon mayonnaise

Grated zest from 1 orange

2–3 teaspoons orange extract

TOPPING

½ cup orange marmalade

½ cup chopped, toasted pecans

1 Line a 9" round cake pan with plastic wrap.

2 In a medium mixing bowl, combine first 6 ingredients for first layer. Beat well.

3 Spread in bottom of prepared pan. Lightly press pecans into first layer.

4 In medium mixing bowl, combine ingredients for second layer. Beat well.

5 Spread over pecans. Cover surface with plastic wrap. Refrigerate 8 hours or up to 3 days.

To Serve

Remove plastic wrap from surface. Invert onto serving platter. Remove pan. Top with orange marmalade and pecans. Serve with gingersnaps and crackers.

Amaretto & Pecan Baked Brie

SERVES 10–12

1 (14–16-ounce) wheel of brie

¾–1 cup chopped pecans

3 tablespoons brown sugar

3 tablespoons amaretto

GARNISHES (OPTIONAL)

Gingersnaps

Apple slices

1 Preheat oven to 350°F.

2 Line jelly-roll pan with foil or parchment. Slice brie in half horizontally, and place on prepared pan.

3 Combine remaining ingredients, and divide over cheese halves.

4 Bake 5–8 minutes until cheese is soft.

To Serve

Serve warm with gingersnaps and apple slices for dipping.

Port Wine & Apple Cheddar Spread

SERVES 10–12

⅓ cup port

1 cup finely chopped dried apple

10 ounces shredded sharp or extra sharp cheddar cheese

1 (8-ounce) package cream cheese, softened

1 teaspoon garlic powder

½ teaspoon salt

¼ teaspoon ground cayenne pepper

In a small bowl, pour port over dried apple. Cover, and let stand at room temperature for several hours or overnight. Combine cheddar, cream cheese and seasonings. Blend well. Add port and apples to mixture. Blend well. Cover with plastic wrap, and refrigerate several hours or up to 1 week before serving.

> **NOTE:** Serve at room temperature with a selection of hearty crackers, toasts and sliced breads. This is a festive and tasty appetizer spread. It's great for autumn picnics and tailgate parties.

Rolled Stuffed Turkey Breast

SERVES 10

STUFFING

2 cups soft bread crumbs

2 garlic cloves, minced

1 tablespoon fresh thyme or
1 teaspoon dried

1 tablespoon minced fresh rosemary
or 1 teaspoon crushed dried

1 teaspoon salt

½ teaspoon freshly ground
black pepper

1 pound uncooked pork sausage,
removed from casing

⅓ cup minced onion

1 egg, beaten

TURKEY

1 (3-pound) whole boneless,
skin-on turkey breast

4 tablespoons butter

¼ cup brandy

Stuffing

Combine first 6 ingredients in a food processor. Process 1 minute.
Transfer bread crumb mixture to a mixing bowl. Add sausage, onion
and egg. Using a sturdy spoon, blend ingredients together.

Turkey

To butterfly whole turkey breast, lay breast flat, skin-side down.
Remove tendons, and trim fat. From center, cut horizontally (parallel
with countertop) through thickest part of each breast side, almost to
outer edge. Fold top pieces outward to enlarge breast. Using the smooth
side of a meat mallet, flatten to more even thickness.

Assembly

1 Preheat oven to 425°F.

2 Evenly distribute stuffing over turkey, leaving a 1" margin. Fold the
extended breast pieces back toward the center. Roll stuffed breast
jelly-roll fashion. Tie securely with kitchen twine at 1" intervals.
Place seam-side down, skin-side up, on rack in roasting pan.

3 Combine melted butter and brandy. Baste turkey.

4 Roast 30 minutes, basting often.

5 Reduce oven to 350°F. Roast 30–40 minutes more, basting often, until meat thermometer registers 170°F.

6 Remove from oven, and let stand 10 minutes. Remove twine, and slice.

FOOD SAFETY GUIDELINES: Never place hot or warm stuffing inside poultry. Do not leave the stuffing inside the turkey for more than 30 minutes before cooking.

Honey-Kissed Hot Apple Cider
with Ginger

MAKES ½ GALLON

½ gallon apple cider

½ cup honey

⅓ cup thinly sliced gingerroot

Combine all ingredients. Heat gently, stirring to dissolve honey, until desired temperature is reached. Strain, and discard ginger. Serve warm.

Hoppin' John New Year's Salad

SERVES 6

2¼ cups cooked Uncle Ben's converted white rice

1½ cups cooked, drained black-eyed peas

¼ cup chopped red onion

¼ cup chopped celery

½ large red bell pepper, seeded, chopped

½ hot pepper (such as jalapeño), seeded, minced

2 tablespoons minced fresh basil

1 garlic clove, minced

Freshly squeezed juice of 1 large lemon

3 tablespoons extra-virgin olive oil

Salt and freshly ground black pepper to taste

Mix together first 8 ingredients. Whisk together remaining ingredients. Stir into salad. Cover, and refrigerate several hours or up to 3 days.

Pepperoni Chips

SERVES 6–8

6 ounces thinly sliced pepperoni

1 cup freshly grated Parmesan cheese

Preheat oven to 350°F. Line a jelly-roll pan with foil or parchment. Arrange pepperoni in a single layer. Sprinkle with Parmesan cheese. Bake 8–10 minutes, until crisp. Drain briefly on paper towels. Serve warm.

> **NOTE:** This is a great snack for game day in front of the television. Everyone loves it, so make plenty!

Chili Bacon Sticks

SERVES 10

20 slices good-quality thinly sliced bacon

20 (8") hard, dry breadsticks

⅓ cup brown sugar

1 tablespoon chili powder

1 Preheat oven to 350°F.

2 Line the bottom part of a broiler pan with foil. Place the food rack part of the broiler pan on top of the foil-lined pan.

3 Wrap a piece of bacon around a breadstick spiral fashion. Repeat.

4 Mix together brown sugar and chili powder. Roll bacon-wrapped breadsticks in brown sugar mixture.

5 Place on broiler rack. Bake 20 minutes.

6 Cool several minutes on pan before removing. Serve at room temperature.

Backyard Lowcountry Seafood Boil

SERVES 8

3 tablespoons shrimp and crab boil
(such as OLD BAY Seasoning)

3 tablespoons salt

1½ gallons water

2 pounds medium red potatoes,
cut into quarters

2 pounds smoked sausage,
cut into 2" pieces

12 ears freshly shucked corn,
broken into 3–4" pieces

4 pounds fresh shrimp

GARNISH

Chopped parsley

> **NOTE:** Do not wait for the liquid to come to a boil when timing
> the sausage, corn and shrimp.

1 In a large stockpot, add shrimp boil and salt to water. Bring to a boil.

2 Add potatoes. Return to a boil, and cook 10 minutes.

3 Add sausage, and cook 5 minutes.

4 Add corn, and cook 5 minutes.

5 Stir in shrimp, and cook 3 minutes. Drain immediately. Garnish
with chopped parsley if desired.

> **NOTE:** Traditionally, this one-dish meal is dumped onto
> a newspaper-lined table set with paper plates and lots of
> paper towels. Serve with butter and loaves of warm, crunchy
> French bread.

Pecan-Crusted Chicken Breasts

with Pralines & Cream Sauce

SERVES 6

CHICKEN

6 boneless, skinless
chicken breast halves

3 cups water

3 tablespoons seasoned salt

3 tablespoons sugar

2 cups all-purpose flour

1 cup finely chopped pecans

1 teaspoon salt

1 teaspoon freshly ground
black pepper

1 teaspoon dried thyme

1 teaspoon dried basil

1 cup milk

1 egg, beaten

¼ cup vegetable oil

¼ cup butter

SAUCE

½ cup chopped pecans

2 cups heavy whipping cream

¼ cup praline liqueur

Salt and freshly ground black pepper
to taste

Chicken

1 Place chicken breast halves in a gallon-size zip-top food storage bag.

2 In a medium mixing bowl, combine water, seasoned salt and sugar;
stir to dissolve. Pour over chicken breast halves, and seal bag,
removing as much air as possible. Let chicken marinate in brine
8–12 hours.

3 Remove chicken from brine, and pat dry.

4 In a shallow container suitable for breading, combine next
6 ingredients.

5 In another shallow container, combine milk and egg.

6 In a large skillet over medium-high heat, heat oil and butter until hot
but not smoking. Dredge each piece of chicken first in dry mixture,
then egg wash, and then again in dry mixture (dry-wet-dry method).
Panfry chicken in skillet until golden brown on both sides, about
7–10 minutes total.

7 Remove chicken from skillet to a platter. Cover with foil to keep warm. Reserve 2 tablespoons of drippings in skillet. Proceed with sauce.

Sauce

In drippings in skillet, sauté pecans over medium-high heat 2 minutes. Add whipping cream and liqueur. Increase heat to high, and bring sauce to a boil. Reduce sauce by half. Season with salt and pepper to taste. Serve warm sauce over chicken.

> **NOTE:** The praline liqueur used in this recipe is an ingredient that is sometimes hard to find in liquor stores. What's a girl to do? Dana Sue shares her own recipe for making your own praline liqueur (see next recipe).

Praline Liqueur

MAKES 10 CUPS. Keep some—share some.

1 pound pecan pieces

1 pound dark brown sugar

3 cups water

4 vanilla beans

4 cups vodka

2 cups brandy

1 cup amaretto

1 Preheat oven to 350°F.

2 Scatter pecan pieces on a baking sheet. Place in center of oven, and bake 8–10 minutes, until pecans release a toasty aroma and are toasted a bit. Do not overcook. Cool to room temperature.

3 Combine brown sugar and 3 cups water in a saucepan. Bring to a boil, stirring to dissolve sugar. Remove from heat.

4 Split vanilla beans lengthwise, and place in a large crock or bowl with the toasted pecans. Pour hot syrup over vanilla beans and pecans. Let cool to room temperature.

5 Add vodka, brandy and amaretto. Stir to blend.

6 Cover airtight with plastic wrap, and let develop at room temperature at least 2 weeks.

7 After 2 weeks, strain liquid through a fine-wire strainer. (For further clarification of liquid, if desired, you can strain the liquid through coffee filters to remove all debris. Because this is a time-consuming process, I normally skip this step.)

8 Pour into bottles, and seal tightly. Attractively label the bottles for gift giving, and store at room temperature.

> **NOTE:** This stuff is absolutely divine. Not only is it the key ingredient for the praline cream sauce for the pecan-crusted chicken breasts recipe, but also it is so delicious when added to coffee or drizzled over pound cake and ice cream. To make a super yummy adult treat, blend with equal parts milk (or half-and-half—how indulgent), and serve over ice. This recipe has won the hearts of all the Sweet Magnolias. Keep some of the liqueur, and share the rest.

Pastel Butter Mints

MAKES 50

1 pound 10X confectioners' sugar

5 tablespoons butter, softened

2 tablespoons cold water

6–12 drops peppermint oil

1 drop food coloring (optional)

Combine all ingredients in a heavy-duty mixer or food processor. Blend until dough comes together and forms a smooth ball. Shape into small balls, and place on waxed paper 1" apart. Flatten with the tines of a fork, dipping in additional confectioners' sugar, if necessary, to prevent sticking. Dry for several hours at room temperature. Store airtight in the refrigerator, or freezer up to 3 months, with wax paper separating the layers.

> **NOTE:** These mints are so delicious, cool and creamy. Serve them at bridal showers, baby showers and weddings. Use food coloring to suit any occasion. Remember to use just a drop or two of the food coloring, keeping the shade subtle.

Erik's Grilled Cheese Panini

with Pecan-Pesto Mayo & Spicy Tomato Jam

MAKES 1

PESTO

⅔ cup pecan halves

1 packed cup fresh basil leaves

½ cup freshly grated Parmesan cheese

2 garlic cloves, minced

⅛ teaspoon ground cayenne pepper

⅓ cup extra-virgin olive oil

Salt to taste

JAM

1 cup sugar

1 cup peeled, finely chopped tomatoes

1 teaspoon freshly grated lemon zest

1 tablespoon lemon juice

¼ teaspoon ground cinnamon

¼ teaspoon allspice

¼ teaspoon cloves

¼ teaspoon cayenne pepper

PANINI

2 slices Italian bread

2 ounces grated smoked mozzarella cheese

2 tablespoons extra-virgin olive oil

1 peeled garlic clove

Pesto

1 Preheat oven to 350°F.

2 Scatter pecans on baking sheet. Bake 8–10 minutes, until nutty smelling. Let cool to room temperature.

3 In the bowl of a food processor, combine pecans, basil, Parmesan, garlic and cayenne. With the machine running, add the olive oil through the top in a steady stream. Season with salt. Refrigerate for use within 2 weeks.

Jam

1 Combine all ingredients in a small saucepan. Bring to a boil, then reduce heat to simmer. Continue to cook, stirring often, until reduced somewhat. Jam will thicken as it cools.

2 Cover, and refrigerate for use within 2 weeks.

Panini

1 Preheat panini press.

2 Place bread slices side by side. On 1 side of 1 slice, smear a liberal amount of pesto. On the other slice, spread jam, and sprinkle on the cheese. Sandwich the 2 slices together. Using a pastry brush, brush the exposed sides of bread slices with olive oil.

3 Place the sandwich on panini press, and close lid, pressing down a bit to slightly weigh down the sandwich. Cook until golden brown and toasted.

4 Remove, and let cool until easily handled. Rub garlic clove over toasted sides. Slice in half on the diagonal.

Chocolate Cloud Cookies

MAKES 18

6 ounces semisweet chocolate chips

3 large egg whites

1 teaspoon pure vanilla extract

½ teaspoon salt

¾ cup sugar

1 cup chopped pecans

1 cup broken vanilla wafers

1 Preheat oven to 350°F.

2 Grease and flour cookie sheets or line them with parchment.

3 Place chocolate chips in microwave-safe dish. Cook at high power until chocolate melts, stirring every 30 seconds. Stir until smooth. Cool slightly.

4 Using an electric mixer, beat egg whites, vanilla and salt until frothy. Gradually beat in sugar until firm peaks hold. Fold in melted chocolate until smooth. Stir in pecans and broken wafers.

5 Drop ¼ cup mounds, 2" apart on prepared pans. Bake 12–15 minutes.

6 Remove from oven. Let cool on pan 5 minutes. Transfer to cooling rack. Cool completely. Store airtight.

Sunburst Lemon Bars

MAKES 48 MINIATURE LEMON BARS, 24 medium or 12 jumbo

CRUST

1 cup butter, softened

½ cup confectioners' sugar

2 cups all-purpose flour

FILLING

2 cups sugar

4 large eggs

⅓ cup flour

Freshly grated zest
of 2 lemons

⅓ cup fresh lemon juice

½ teaspoon baking powder

GARNISH

Confectioners' sugar

Crust

1 Preheat oven to 350°F.

2 Cream butter and sugar together in a mixing bowl. Add flour all at once, and mix until thoroughly combined.

3 Place in a parchment-lined 9" × 13" × 2" metal baking pan, and press evenly to cover entire bottom. (**Note:** I often place a piece of plastic wrap on top of the dough when pressing it out to keep the dough from sticking to my hands.)

4 Bake 20 minutes. Prepare the filling during the last 5 minutes of the crust baking.

Filling

1 Combine all filling ingredients, and mix well.

2 Remove crust from oven. Pour filling over baked crust, return to the oven, and bake an additional 33–35 minutes.

3 Remove pan from the oven, and let cool completely on a cooling rack.

4 When cooled, lift out of the pan by the overhanging parchment paper, and place on a cutting board. Trim off edges with a large, long sharp knife, and discard (chef's treat!). Cut into squares of desirable size. Dust tops with confectioners' sugar.

Fall Festival Munch Mix

MAKES 20 CUPS

1 pound miniature pretzels

1 pound roasted, salted peanuts

1 (12-ounce) box original flavor cheese cracker squares (such as Cheese Nips)

1 (9½-ounce) box miniature buttery crackers filled with peanut butter (such as Ritz Bits)

¾ cup butter

1 packed cup light brown sugar

½ cup light corn syrup

2 teaspoons vanilla extract

1 (1-pound) bag candy-coated peanut butter candies (such as Reese's Pieces)

2 (12-ounce) bags candy corn

1 Preheat oven to 250°F.

2 Using a nonstick cooking spray, coat a very large roasting pan or disposable foil pan. Combine first 4 ingredients in prepared pan.

3 In a medium saucepan, melt butter. Add brown sugar and corn syrup. Bring to a boil, stirring occasionally. Boil 5 minutes.

4 Remove from heat. Whisk in vanilla. Pour over pretzel blend. Stir gently to coat.

5 Bake 1 hour, stirring once every 15 minutes.

6 Place on a cooling rack. Stir several times during cooling to avoid clumps. Once cooled, stir in candies. Store airtight.

> **NOTE:** This recipe makes 20 cups!! You may be asking yourself, What am I going to do with 20 cups of this party mix? Be warned: This stuff magically disappears. It's a favorite of the Sweet Magnolias and our families.

Old-Fashioned Molasses Cookies

MAKES 100

1½ cups sugar

1 cup butter, softened

1 cup molasses

2 eggs, beaten

4 cups all-purpose flour

4 teaspoons baking soda

2 teaspoons cinnamon

1 teaspoon salt

1 teaspoon ground ginger

Additional sugar

1 Preheat oven to 350°F.

2 In a large mixing bowl, cream sugar and butter until light and fluffy. Add molasses and eggs; blend well.

3 In a medium mixing bowl, whisk together flour, baking soda, cinnamon, salt and ginger.

4 Add dry ingredients to the creamed mixture. Blend until well incorporated.

5 Shape tablespoons of dough into balls, and coat in sugar. Place 2" apart on parchment-lined or greased baking sheets. Flatten tops slightly.

6 Bake 10–12 minutes.

Conversion Charts

WEIGHT

1 ounce	28 grams	12 ounces or ¾ pound	340 grams
4 ounces or ¼ pound	113 grams	1 pound or 16 ounces	450 grams
⅓ pound	150 grams	2 pounds	900 grams
8 ounces or ½ pound	230 grams	2.2 pounds	1 kilogram
⅔ pound	300 grams		

TEMPERATURE

FAHRENHEIT	CELSIUS	FAHRENHEIT	CELSIUS
212°	100°	375°	190°
250°	120°	400°	200°
275°	140°	425°	220°
300°	150°	450°	230°
325°	160°	475°	240°
350°	180°	500°	260°

VOLUME

1 teaspoon	5 milliliters	¾ cup or 6 fluid ounces	180 milliliters
1 tablespoon or ½ fluid ounce	15 milliliters	1 cup or 8 fluid ounces or ½ pint	240 milliliters
⅛ cup or 1 fluid ounce	30 milliliters	1½ cups or 12 fluid ounces	350 milliliters
¼ cup or 2 fluid ounces	60 milliliters	2 cups or 16 fluid ounces or 1 pint	475 milliliters
⅓ cup	80 milliliters	3 cups or 1½ pints	700 milliliters
½ cup or 4 fluid ounces	120 milliliters	4 cups or 2 pints or 1 quart	950 milliliters
⅔ cup	160 milliliters	4 quarts or 1 gallon	3.8 liters

About the Authors

With her roots firmly planted in the South, **SHERRYL WOODS** has written many of her more than 100 books in that distinctive setting, whether in her home state of Virginia, her adopted state, Florida, or her much-adored South Carolina. She is the *New York Times* and *USA TODAY* bestselling author of the Sweet Magnolias series and is best known for her ability to create endearing small-town communities and families. She divides her time between her childhood summer home overlooking the Potomac River in Colonial Beach, Virginia, and her oceanfront condo in Jacksonville Beach, Florida. Visit her at SherrylWoods.com.

TEDDI WOHLFORD is the chef and owner of Culinary Creations in Macon, Georgia. Her catering company offers a unique assortment of Southern cuisine. She specializes in fare that she calls "uptown down South," updated and upscale versions of timeless Southern classics. Teddi is the Fine Foods Writer for the *Telegraph* (Macon, Georgia) and a frequent guest chef on 13WMAZ television. With family in the upstate of South Carolina and in-laws in the Lowcountry, Teddi spends as much time as possible in her "heart's home" of South Carolina and travels the South teaching gourmet cooking classes.

Index

— A —

Agave nectar, 3
Alcoholic beverages. *See*
 Beverages, alcoholic
Almonds
 Biscotti, 170–71
 Chicken Salad with Dijon-
  Dill Dressing & Toasted
  Almonds, 94
 Chocolate Amaretto Cake
  (no sugar added), 155
 Dana Sue's Almond-Filled
  Croissants, 76, 79
 Iced Almond-Lemonade Tea,
  184–85
 Southern-Style Green Beans
  Amandine with Frizzled Bacon
  & Smoked Almonds, 50
Amaretto
 Chocolate Cake
  (no sugar added), 155
 Pecan Baked Brie with, 194
Ambrosia, Southern Christmas,
 110
Apples
 Bread Pudding with Cinnamon
  Ice Cream & Caramel Sauce, 141
 Chunky Apple Bran Muffins
  (fat-free), 168–69
 Deep-Dish Pie with Crunchy
  Crumb Topping, 146–47
 Fresh Apple Cake, 60–61
 Honey-Kissed Hot Cider with
  Ginger, 197
 pie spice, 60
 Port Wine & Apple Cheddar
  Spread, 195
 Salad with Sherry & Honey
  Vinaigrette, 65
 Southern Christmas
  Ambrosia, 110
 Southern Legacy Apple & Mint
  Spritzer (no sugar added), 166

Asparagus
 Sea Bass with Vegetables
  & Herbs en Papillote, 28–29
 Vegetarian Pasta Primavera with
  Smoked Gouda Sauce, 45
Avocado, Dana Sue's Killer
 Chunky Guacamole, 4–5

— B —

Backyard Lowcountry Seafood
 Boil, 200–201
Bacon
 Caramelized Onion & Bacon
  Quiche, 103
 Carolina Red Rice, 51
 Chili Bacon Sticks, 199
 Southern-Style Green Beans
  Amandine with Frizzled
  Bacon & Smoked Almonds,
  50
 Sullivan's Smothered Corn
  with Frizzled Bacon, 75
 & Swiss Appetizer
  Cheesecake, 19
Balsamic Vinaigrette (fat-free), 174
Barbecue Salad with Tangy
 Coleslaw, 96
Bars
 Dulce De Leche Cheesecake, 115
 Sunburst Lemon, 210–11
Basil
 Erik's Grilled Cheese Panini
  with Pecan-Pesto Mayo &
  Spicy Tomato Jam, 206
 Strawberry & Basil
  Vinaigrette, 173
 Sweet & Tangy Tomato-Basil
  Vinaigrette, 33
Beans
 Black, Chili, 124–25
 Navy, Soup, 22
 Roasted Corn & Mixed Bean
  Salsa, 126

Beverages, alcoholic
 Citrus Bourbon Slushy, 8
 Frosted Café Royale, 82
 Helen's Lethal Margaritas, 3
 Magnolia Blossom Cocktail, 6
 Mint Juleps, 7
 Mulled Wine Punch, 191
 Poinsettia Punch, 180
 Praline Liqueur, 204
 simple syrup for, 6
 Snow Cream Martinis, 6
 White Sangria, 182
Beverages, non-alcoholic
 Christmas Festival Eggnog,
  176, 179
 Cucumber Cooler, 164–65
 Front Porch Sippin' Lemonade,
  183
 Fuzzy Navel Smoothie, 167
 Golden Wassail, 181
 Honey-Kissed Hot Apple Cider
  with Ginger, 197
 Hot Cocoa, 186–87
 Iced Almond-Lemonade Tea,
  184–85
 Southern Legacy Apple & Mint
  Spritzer (no sugar added), 166
Biscotti, Almond, 170–71
Biscuits
 baking mix for, 104
 Petite Dilly, 104
 Sweet Potato, 105
 Whipping Cream Drop, 106
Black Bean Chili, 124–25
Black-eyed peas, Hoppin' John
 New Year's Salad, 198
Blue Cheese
 Apple Salad with Sherry &
  Honey Vinaigrette, 65
 Baby Greens with Pears &
  Toasted Walnut Vinaigrette, 26
 Dressing with Cognac, 13
 Lavender Blue Dilly Dilly Green
  Bean Salad, 64

Bran Muffins, Chunky Apple (fat-free), 168–69
Bread Pudding
  Baked Apple with Cinnamon Ice Cream & Caramel Sauce, 141
  Cinnamon Roll with Whipped Vanilla Bean Crème, 140
Broccoli, Crustless Three-Cheese Quiche with, 102
Brownies, Warm Walnut à la Mode with Hot Fudge Sauce, 150–51
Butter
  Browned, & Lemon Sauce, 38
  Cranberry-Orange, 87
  Pastel Butter Mints, 205
Buttermilk-Glazed Carrot Cake with Orange Cream Cheese Frosting, 136–37
Butternut squash, Fall Harvest Bisque, 72–73

— C —

Cabbage, Barbecue Salad with Tangy Coleslaw, 96
Cakes. See also Cheesecake
  Buttermilk-Glazed Carrot, with Orange Cream Cheese Frosting, 136–37
  Chocolate Amaretto (no sugar added), 155
  Fresh Apple, 60–61
  Pumpkin Roll, 142–43
  Southern Cream Cheese Pound, 130, 139
  Southern Supreme Red Velvet, 134–35
  Tres Leches, 128–29
  Valentine's Special Decadence (flourless), 148–49
Canapés, Vidalia Onion, 63
Candy
  Candied Orange Peel, 152–53
  Chocolate Sugarplum Truffles, 144–45
  Homemade Marshmallows, 188–89
  Jingle Bell Candied Cranberries, 109
  Pastel Butter Mints, 205
  Southern Pecan Toffee, 154

Carolina Gold Rice, 28–29
Carolina Red Rice, 51
Carolina Rémoulade Sauce, 99
Carrots
  Buttermilk-Glazed Cake with Orange Cream Cheese Frosting, 136–37
  Corner Spa Cream of Carrot Soup (low-fat), 162–63
  Sea Bass with Vegetables & Herbs en Papillote, 28–29
  Vegetarian Pasta Primavera with Smoked Gouda Sauce, 45
Catfish, Panfried with Spicy Cornmeal Coating, 36–37
Cauliflower, Vegetarian Pasta Primavera with Smoked Gouda Sauce, 45
Cheddar
  Blossoms, 12
  Corn Muffins, 21
  Port Wine & Apple Spread, 195
Cheese
  Amaretto & Pecan Baked Brie, 194
  Apple Salad with Sherry & Honey Vinaigrette, 65
  Baby Greens with Pears, Blue Cheese & Toasted Walnut Vinaigrette, 26
  Bacon & Swiss Appetizer Cheesecake, 19
  Blue Cheese Dressing with Cognac, 13
  Caramelized Onion & Bacon Quiche, 103
  Cheddar Blossoms, 12
  Cheddar Corn Muffins, 21
  Country Ham & Grits Quiche with Red-Eye Gravy, 100–101
  Crustless Broccoli & Three-Cheese Quiche, 102
  Erik's Grilled Cheese Panini with Pecan-Pesto Mayo & Spicy Tomato Jam, 206–7
  Herb, Spread, 30
  Jacked-Up Tex-Mex Macaroni &, 118

Lavender Blue Dilly Dilly Green Bean Salad, 64
  Orange & Toasted Pecan Appetizer Torte, 193
  Port Wine & Apple Cheddar Spread, 195
  Shrimp, Crab & Swiss Appetizer Cheesecake, 20
  Smoked Gouda Sauce, 45
  Stuffed French Toast with Glazed Strawberries, 91
  Three-Cheese Macaroni Casserole, 48–49
  Uptown Down-South Grits, 111
Cheesecake
  Bacon & Swiss Appetizer, 19
  cracker crust, 127
  Dulce De Leche Bars, 115
  Shrimp, Crab & Swiss Appetizer, 20
  Tex-Mex Appetizer, 127
Chicken
  Caesar Salad Wraps, 172
  C'mon, Baby, Light My Fire Wings, 10–11
  Corner Spa Tortilla Soup (low-fat), 159
  Enchilada Casserole with Speedy Mole Sauce, 116–17
  Gold Nugget Chicken & Pasta Salad, 175
  "Oven-Fried" Tenders, 43
  Peachy Grilled, with Spicy Peanut Sauce, 39
  Pecan-Crusted Breasts with Pralines & Cream Sauce, 202–3
  Pineapple Chicken Salad, 95
  Salad with Dijon-Dill Dressing & Toasted Almonds, 94
Chicken Wings
  Blue Cheese Dressing with Cognac for, 13
  C'mon, Baby, Light My Fire Wings, 10–11
Chili
  Bacon Sticks, 199
  Black Bean, 124–25
Chocolate
  Amaretto Cake (no sugar added), 155

Cloud Cookies, 208–9
Hot Cocoa, 186–87
Pluff Mud Fudgy Bottom Peanut
  Butter Icebox Pie, 133
Speedy Mole Sauce, 116–17
Sugarplum Truffles, 144–45
Valentine's Special Decadence
  Cake (flourless), 148–49
Warm Walnut Brownie
  à la Mode with Hot Fudge
  Sauce, 150–51
Chowder, Southern Smothered
  Corn, 68–69
Christmas Festival Eggnog
  (alcohol-free), 176, 179
Cinnamon Roll Bread Pudding
  with Whipped Vanilla Bean
  Crème, 140
Citrus Bourbon Slushy, 8
Coating (for meat, fish, or
  vegetables)
  Bread Crumb-Herb-Nut
    Mixture, 42
  Cornmeal, 36–37, 70
  Cracker, 43
  dry-wet-dry method, 70
Cocktail, Magnolia Blossom, 6
Coconut Cream Tart in Pecan
  Shortbread Crust, 138
Coffee, Frosted Café Royale, 82
Coleslaw, Tangy, 96
Conversion charts, 214
Cookies
  Almond Biscotti, 170–71
  Chocolate Cloud, 208–9
  Old-Fashioned Molasses, 213
Corn
  Backyard Lowcountry
    Seafood Boil, 200–201
  Cheddar Muffins, 21
  Muffin Mix, 21
  Roasted Corn & Mixed Bean
    Salsa, 126
  Southern Smothered Corn
    Chowder, 68–69
  Sullivan's Smothered Corn
    with Frizzled Bacon, 75
Corner Spa Cream of Carrot Soup
  (low-fat), 162–63
Corner Spa Tortilla Soup (low-fat),
  159

Cornmeal
  Coating (for fish), 36–37
  Corn Muffin Mix, 21
  Crusted Fried Okra, 70–71
Country Ham & Grits Quiche
  with Red-Eye Gravy, 100–101
Crab
  Crabgrass, 190
  Lowcountry Hash, 89
  Lowcountry Seafood Gumbo, 67
  Lowcountry She-Crab Soup, 23
  Shrimp & Swiss Appetizer
    Cheesecake, 20
  Sullivan's Crab Cakes, 97
Crabgrass, 190
Cranberries
  Jingle Bell Candied, 109
  Orange Butter, 87
  Orange Scones with Orange
    Glaze, 84–85
Croissants, Dana Sue's Almond-
  Filled, 76, 79
Crumb Topping, 27
Cucumber Cooler, 164–65

— D —

Dates, Macaroon Muffins with
  Pecans &, 88
Dill. See also Pickles/pickled foods
  Dijon-Dill Dressing, 94
  Dressing, 64
  Lavender Blue Dilly Dilly Green
    Bean Salad, 64
  Petite Dilly Biscuits, 104
  Pickled Dilly Green Beans, 59
Dulce De Leche Cheesecake Bars,
  115

— E —

Eggnog (alcohol-free), 176, 179
Enchilada Casserole, Chicken with
  Speedy Mole Sauce, 116–17
Erik's Grilled Cheese Panini with
  Pecan-Pesto Mayo & Spicy
  Tomato Jam, 206–7

— F —

Fall Festival Munch Mix, 212

Fish
  Bourbon & Brown Sugar Grilled
    Salmon with Tropical Fruit
    Salsa, 31–32
  Citrus Salmon with Crunchy
    Crumb Topping, 27
  Lowcountry Seafood Gumbo, 67
  Panfried Catfish with Spicy
    Cornmeal Coating, 36–37
  Pan-Seared Trout with Browned
    Butter & Lemon Sauce, 38
  Sea Bass with Vegetables &
    Herbs en Papillote, 28–29
French Toast, Stuffed, with Glazed
  Strawberries, 91
Front Porch Sippin' Lemonade, 183
Frostings and icings
  butter icing for Southern Red
    Velvet Cake, 134–35
  Orange Cream Cheese, 136–37
Fuzzy Navel Smoothie, 167

— G —

Garlic
  & Rosemary Roasted Pork Loin
    with Sour Cream &
    Mushroom Sauce, 44
  & Rosemary Rub (for pork), 44
  Toast Rounds, 18
Gazpacho, Summer, 156, 160
Ginger, Honey-Kissed Hot Apple
  Cider with, 197
Gingerbread Scones, 86
Glazes
  buttermilk, 136–37
  chocolate, 148–49
Golden Wassail (alcohol-free), 181
Gold Nugget Chicken & Pasta
  Salad, 175
Grapes
  Pineapple Chicken Salad, 94
  Southern Christmas Ambrosia,
    110
Gravy
  Country Ham Cream-Style,
    92–93
  Red-Eye, 100
Green Beans
  Lavender Blue Dilly Dilly Salad,
    64

Pickled Dilly, 59
Southern-Style Amandine
with Frizzled Bacon & Smoked
Almonds, 50
Grits
Country Ham & Grits Quiche
with Red-Eye Gravy, 100–101
Creamy Yellow, 92–93
Uptown Down-South Cheese,
111
Guacamole, 4–5
Gullah Peanut & Sweet Potato
Soup, 24

— **H** —

Ham
Country Ham & Grits Quiche
with Red-Eye Gravy, 100–101
Country Ham Cream-Style
Gravy, 92–93
Southern Seafood Paella, 122–23
Helen's Lethal Margaritas, 3
Herb Cheese Spread, 30
Hollandaise Sauce, Sherry, 98
Honey Grilled Pork Tenderloin
with Peach Salsa, 40–41
Honey-Kissed Hot Apple Cider
with Ginger, 197
Hoppin' John New Year's Salad, 198
Hot Cocoa, 186–87

— **I** —

Iced Almond-Lemonade Tea,
184–85
Icings. *See* Frostings and icings

— **J** —

Jacked-Up Tex-Mex Macaroni
& Cheese, 118
Jalapeño peppers
caution regarding, 126
Pico de Gallo, 119
Roasted Corn & Mixed Bean
Salsa, 126
Toasted Pecan & Red Pepper
Jam, 17
Jams
Peach Cobbler, 108

Spicy Tomato, 206–7
Strawberry Preserves with Rose
Geranium & Vanilla Essence,
107
Toasted Pecan & Red Pepper, 17
Jingle Bell Candied Cranberries,
109

— **K** —

Kiwi, Tropical Fruit Salsa, 31–32

— **L** —

Lamb, Roasted Spring, with Herbs
& Madeira Sauce, 42–43
Lavender Blue Dilly Dilly Green
Bean Salad, 64
Lemon
Microwave Curd, 90
& Poppy Seed Scones, 83
Sunburst Bars, 210–11
Lemonade
Front Porch Sippin', 183
Iced Almond-Lemonade Tea,
184–85
Lowcountry Crab Hash, 89
Lowcountry Seafood Gumbo, 67
Lowcountry She-Crab Soup, 23

— **M** —

Macaroni & Cheese
Jacked-Up Tex-Mex, 118
Three-Cheese Macaroni
Casserole, 48–49
Macaroon
Fresh Peach Tarts, 74
Muffins with Dates & Pecans,
88
MAGGI liquid seasoning, 162
Mango
Helen's Lethal Margaritas, 3
Tropical Fruit Salsa, 31–32
Margaritas, Helen's Lethal, 3
Marinade (for salmon), 31–32
Marshmallows, Homemade,
188–89
Martinis, Snow Cream, 6
Microwave Lemon Curd, 90
Mint
Juleps, 7

Pastel Butter Mints, 205
Spritzer, Southern Legacy Apple
& Mint (no sugar added), 166
Molasses Cookies, 213
Muffins
Cheddar Corn, 21
Chunky Apple Bran (fat-free),
168–69
Corn Muffin Mix, 21
Macaroon with Dates & Pecans,
88
Mulled Wine Punch, 191
Mushrooms
Mixed Mushroom Risotto,
46–47
Sherried Mushroom Soup, 25
Sour Cream & Mushroom
Sauce, 44
Vegetarian Pasta Primavera with
Smoked Gouda Sauce, 45
Mussels, Southern Seafood Paella,
122–23

— **N** —

Navy Bean Soup, 22
Non-alcoholic beverages. *See*
Beverages, non-alcoholic
Nuts. *See* Almonds; Pecans;
Walnuts

— **O** —

Oatmeal, Pecan & Oat Streusel
Topping, 52
Okra
Cornmeal-Crusted, 70–71
Dana Sue's Pickled, 58
Onions
Caramelized Onion & Bacon
Quiche, 103
Pico de Gallo, 119
Vidalia, Canapés, 63
Vidalia, Vinaigrette (fat-free), 161
Oranges
Candied Orange Peel, 152–53
Cranberry-Orange Butter, 87
Cranberry-Orange Scones with
Orange Glaze, 84–85
Cream Cheese Frosting, 136–37
Fuzzy Navel Smoothie, 167

Orange & Toasted Pecan Appetizer Torte, 193

Southern Christmas Ambrosia, 110

— P —

Panini, Erik's Grilled Cheese, 206–7

Pan-Seared Trout with Browned Butter & Lemon Sauce, 38

Pasta
  Gold Nugget Chicken & Pasta Salad, 175
  Jacked-Up Tex-Mex Macaroni & Cheese, 118
  Shrimp Scampi Linguine, 34–35
  Three-Cheese Macaroni Casserole, 48–49
  Vegetarian Primavera with Smoked Gouda Sauce, 45

Pastel Butter Mints, 205

Peaches
  Cobbler Jam, 108
  Fresh Peach Macaroon Tarts, 74
  Fuzzy Navel Smoothie, 167
  Peachy Grilled Chicken with Spicy Peanut Sauce, 39
  Salsa, 41

Peanut butter
  Gullah Peanut & Sweet Potato Soup, 24
  Pluff Mud Fudgy Bottom Icebox Pie, 133
  Spicy Peanut Sauce, 39

Pears, Baby Greens with Blue Cheese & Toasted Walnut Vinaigrette, 26

Peas
  Black-eyed, Hoppin' John New Year's Salad, 198
  Spring, Vichyssoise with Vegetable Confetti, 62

Pecans
  Amaretto & Pecan Baked Brie, 194
  Chocolate Cloud Cookies, 208–9
  Coconut Cream Tart in Shortbread Crust, 138
  Crusted Chicken Breasts with Pralines & Cream Sauce, 202–3

Macaroon Muffins with Dates & Pecans, 88

Orange & Toasted Pecan Appetizer Torte, 193

Pesto with, 206–7

Praline Liqueur, 204

Southern Christmas Ambrosia, 110

Southern Pecan Toffee, 154

Sweet Potato Soufflé with Pecan & Oat Streusel Topping, 52

Toasted, and Red Pepper Jam, 17

Pepperoni Chips, 198

Peppers (red or green bell). See also Jalapeño peppers
  Confetti, 62
  Toasted Pecan & Red Pepper Jam, 17

Pesto, 206–7

Petite Dilly Biscuits, 104

Pickles/pickled foods
  Dana Sue's Pickled Okra, 58
  Fire & Ice Pickles, 9
  Pickled Dilly Green Beans, 59
  Pickled Green Tomatoes, 57
  Spicy Pickled Shrimp, 192

Pico de Gallo, 119

Pies
  Deep-Dish Apple with Crunchy Crumb Topping, 146–47
  Pluff Mud Fudgy Bottom Peanut Butter Icebox, 133

Pie spice, apple, 60

Pineapple
  Chicken Salad, 95
  Southern Christmas Ambrosia, 110
  Tropical Fruit Salsa, 31–32

Poinsettia Punch, 180

Poppy Seed, Lemon &, Scones, 83

Pork
  Barbecue Salad with Tangy Coleslaw, 96
  Garlic & Rosemary Roasted, with Sour Cream & Mushroom Sauce, 44
  Honey Grilled Tenderloin with Peach Salsa, 40–41
  rub for, 44

Smoky Pork-Filled Tamales, 112, 120–21

Potatoes. See also Sweet Potatoes
  Backyard Lowcountry Seafood Boil, 200–201
  Lowcountry Crab Hash, 89
  Southern Smothered Corn Chowder, 68–69
  Spring Pea Vichyssoise with Vegetable Confetti, 62
  Walnut-Crusted, with Herbs, 53

Pound Cake, 130, 139

Praline Liqueur, 204

Pumpkin Cake Roll, 142–43

— Q —

Quiche
  Caramelized Onion & Bacon, 103
  Country Ham & Grits with Red-Eye Gravy, 100–101
  Crustless Broccoli & Three-Cheese, 102

— R —

Red Velvet Cake, 134–35

Rice
  Carolina Gold, 28–29
  Carolina Red, 51
  "converted," 51
  Hoppin' John New Year's Salad, 198
  Mixed Mushroom Risotto, 46–47

Risotto, Mixed Mushroom, 46–47

— S —

Salad dressings
  for Ambrosia, 110
  Balsamic Vinaigrette (fat-free), 174
  Blue Cheese with Cognac, 13
  cream cheese-mayonnaise (for chicken salad), 95
  Dijon-Dill, 94
  Dill, 64
  Sherry & Honey Vinaigrette, 65

Strawberry & Basil Vinaigrette, 173

Sweet & Tangy Tomato-Basil Vinaigrette, 33

Toasted Walnut Vinaigrette, 26

Vidalia Onion Vinaigrette (fat-free), 161

Salads
Apple, with Sherry & Honey Vinaigrette, 65

Baby Greens with Pears, Blue Cheese & Toasted Walnut Vinaigrette, 26

Barbecue with Tangy Coleslaw, 96

Chicken, with Dijon-Dill Dressing & Toasted Almonds, 94

Chicken Caesar Wraps, 172

Gold Nugget Chicken & Pasta, 175

Hoppin' John New Year's, 198

Lavender Blue Dilly Dilly Green Bean, 64

Mixed with Strawberry & Basil Vinaigrette, 173

Oven-Roasted Sweet Potato Tailgate, 66

Pineapple Chicken, 95

Southern Christmas Ambrosia, 110

Salmon
Bourbon & Brown Sugar Grilled, with Tropical Fruit Salsa, 31–32

Citrus, with Crunchy Crumb Topping, 27

Salsa
Peach, 41

Pico de Gallo, 119

Roasted Corn & Mixed Bean, 126

Tropical Fruit, 31–32

Sangria, White, 182

Sauces
Browned Butter & Lemon, 38

Caramel, 141

Carolina Rémoulade, 99

Herbs & Madeira Sauce, 42-43

Hot Fudge, 150–51

Pralines & Cream, 202–3

Scampi, 35

Sherry Hollandaise, 98

Smoked Gouda, 45

Sour Cream & Mushroom, 44

Speedy Mole, 116–17

Spicy Peanut, 39

Tamale, 120–21

Sausage
Backyard Lowcountry Seafood Boil, 200–201

Black Bean Chili, 124–25

Jacked-Up Tex-Mex Macaroni & Cheese, 118

Southern Seafood Paella, 122–23

Spicy Shrimp & Sausage with Country Ham Cream-Style Gravy over Creamy Yellow Grits, 92–93

Scallops, Southern Seafood Paella, 122–23

Scones
Classic Cream, 80–81

Cranberry-Orange with Orange Glaze, 84–85

Gingerbread, 86

Lemon & Poppy Seed, 83

Sea Bass with Vegetables & Herbs en Papillote, 28–29

Seafood. See also Fish
Backyard Lowcountry Boil, 200–201

Lowcountry Crab Hash, 89

Lowcountry Gumbo, 67

Lowcountry She-Crab Soup, 23

Shrimp, Crab & Swiss Appetizer Cheesecake, 20

Shrimp Scampi Linguine, 34–35

Southern Paella, 122–23

Spicy Pickled Shrimp, 192

Spicy Shrimp & Sausage with Country Ham Cream-Style Gravy over Creamy Yellow Grits, 92–93

Sherried Mushroom Soup, 25

Sherry Hollandaise Sauce, 98

Shrimp
Backyard Lowcountry Seafood Boil, 200–201

Crab & Swiss Appetizer Cheesecake, 20

Lowcountry Seafood Gumbo, 67

Scampi Linguine, 34–35

Southern Seafood Paella, 122–23

Spicy Pickled Shrimp, 192

Spicy Shrimp & Sausage with Country Ham Cream-Style Gravy over Creamy Yellow Grits, 92–93

Simple syrup, 6

Smoothies, Fuzzy Navel, 167

Snacks
Cheddar Blossoms, 12

Chili Bacon Sticks, 199

Fall Festival Munch Mix, 212

Pepperoni Chips, 198

Soufflé, Sweet Potato with Pecan & Oat Streusel Topping, 52

Soups
Corner Spa Cream of Carrot (low-fat), 162–63

Corner Spa Tortilla (low-fat), 159

Fall Harvest Bisque, 72–73

Gullah Peanut & Sweet Potato, 24

Lowcountry She-Crab, 23

Navy Bean, 22

Sherried Mushroom, 25

Southern Smothered Corn Chowder, 68–69

Spring Pea Vichyssoise with Vegetable Confetti, 62

Summer Gazpacho, 156, 160

Sour Cream & Mushroom Sauce, 44

Southern Christmas Ambrosia, 110

Southern Cream Cheese Pound Cake, 130, 139

Southern Legacy Apple & Mint Spritzer (no sugar added), 166

Southern Pecan Toffee, 154

Southern Seafood Paella, 122–23

Southern Smothered Corn Chowder, 68–69

Southern-Style Green Beans Amandine with Frizzled Bacon & Smoked Almonds, 50

Southern Supreme Red Velvet
Cake, 134–35
Spinach, Crabgrass, 190
Spreads
Herb Cheese, 30
Port Wine & Apple Cheddar,
195
Squash (summer), Sea Bass with
Vegetables & Herbs en Papillote,
28–29
Squash (winter), Fall Harvest
Bisque, 72–73
Strawberries
Helen's Lethal Margaritas, 3
Preserves with Rose Geranium
& Vanilla Essence, 107
Strawberry & Basil Vinaigrette,
173
Stuffed French Toast with
Glazed Strawberries, 91
Stuffing, 196–97
Sullivan's Crab Cakes, 97
Sullivan's Smothered Corn with
Frizzled Bacon, 75
Sunburst Lemon Bars, 210–11
Sweet Potatoes
Biscuits, 105
Gullah Peanut & Sweet Potato
Soup, 24
Oven-Roasted, Tailgate Salad, 66
Soufflé with Pecan & Oat
Streusel Topping, 52

— T —

Tamales, Smoky Pork-Filled, 112,
120-121
Tarts
Coconut Cream in Pecan
Shortbread Crust, 138
Fresh Peach Macaroon, 74
macaroon crust, 74
Tex-Mex Appetizer Cheesecake,
127

Toffee, Southern Pecan, 154
Tomatoes
Carolina Red Rice, 51
Corner Spa Tortilla Soup
(low-fat), 159
Pickled Green, 57
Pico de Gallo, 119
Speedy Mole Sauce, 116–17
Spicy Jam, 206–7
Summer Gazpacho, 156, 160
Sweet & Tangy, Basil
Vinaigrette, 33
Toppings
Crunchy Crumb, 146–47
Microwave Lemon Curd, 90
Orange Glaze, 84
Pecan & Oat Streusel, 52
sugarless almond whipped
cream, 155
Walnut-Crust, 53
Whipped Cream, 74, 128–29,
155
Whipped Vanilla Bean Crème,
140
Tortillas
Chicken Caesar Salad Wraps,
172
Corner Spa Soup (low-fat), 159
Tres Leches Cake, 128–29
Trout, Pan-Seared with Browned
Butter & Lemon Sauce, 38
Truffles, Chocolate Sugarplum,
144–45
Turkey, Rolled Stuffed Breast,
196–97

— V —

Valentine's Special Decadence
Cake (flourless), 148–49
Vegetables. See also specific
vegetables
dry-wet-dry coating method,
70

Pasta Primavera with Smoked
Gouda Sauce, 45
Sea Bass & Herbs en Papillote,
with, 28-29
Spring Pea Vichyssoise with
Vegetable Confetti, 62
Vichyssoise, Spring Pea with
Vegetable Confetti, 62
Vidalia Onions
Canapés, 63
Vinaigrette (fat-free), 161
Vinaigrette
Balsamic (fat-free), 174
Sherry & Honey, 65
Strawberry & Basil, 173
Sweet & Tangy Tomato-Basil, 33
Toasted Walnut, 26
Vidalia Onion (fat-free), 161

— W —

Walnuts
Brownie à la Mode with Hot
Fudge Sauce, 150–51
Toasted, Vinaigrette, 26
Walnut-Crusted Potatoes with
Herbs, 53
Whipped Cream, 13, 23, 25, 45, 46,
52, 62, 73, 74, 81, 83, 84, 86, 92,
106, 111, 128–29, 133, 140, 145,
148, 155
Whipping Cream Drop Biscuits,
106
White Sangria, 182
Wraps, Chicken Caesar Salad,
172

— Z —

Zucchini
Sea Bass with Vegetables
& Herbs en Papillote, 28–29
Vegetarian Pasta Primavera
with Smoked Gouda Sauce, 45